Nora Mae,

a Remarkable,

Insignificant Person

by Alice Hein Schiel B.S., M.Ed

xulon PRESS

Contents

Introduction

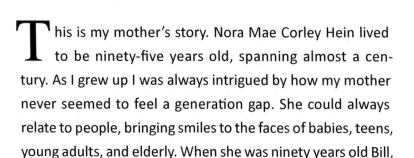

This is my mother's story. Nora Mae Corley Hein lived to be ninety-five years old, spanning almost a century. As I grew up I was always intrigued by how my mother never seemed to feel a generation gap. She could always relate to people, bringing smiles to the faces of babies, teens, young adults, and elderly. When she was ninety years old Bill, Benjamin, and I took her out to eat. A gentleman probably in his sixties walked over to our table.

"Nora Mae, we are having a surprise birthday party for (someone) on Saturday. Would you sing for us at the party?" he asked.

Mom thought for a moment and then slowly nodded, "On Saturday? Okay, I will. Let me know the details."

He smiled broadly and added, "We will, and thanks!" He walked briskly out of the restaurant.

She had made his day. At 90 years old she was still warming people's hearts. She continued to sing for friends who often remarked that she had the voice of an angel.

Mom's story has historical significance in that it documents true accounts of a family's life during peace, joy, and prosperity, as well as during war, sorrow, and financial depression. It provides a glimpse into love and the depths it will go. Mom lived 89 of her 95 years in Burleson County, Texas so her story is intertwined with the history of that county. She is "insignificant" in the fact that her name is not yet known by millions. She had no earthly fame. This book reveals how she gave to the community she loved, becoming the bridge that allowed many others to cross from good ideas to action.

My mother's life was remarkable. More than thirty years ago I told her that I wanted to write a book about her someday. She began to randomly make notes for me which I stuck into a file. When mom died in 2011 she left a small notebook with this inscription, "Give this to Alice." The time has come. I have spent the past year compiling this book with you, the reader, in mind. I hope that you will cry; I hope that you will laugh; I hope that your life will be enriched by the Nora Mae you encounter in these pages.

This is my mother's story.

Dedication

This book is dedicated to John Pinkerton, English teacher at Somerville High School, who once told me that I could write and to Dr. P.E. Parotti, English professor at Sam Houston State University, who tried to convince me to major in English. Your encouragements long ago fueled my determination to complete this book.

Acknowledgments

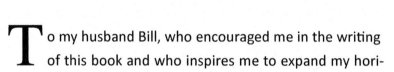

To my husband Bill, who encouraged me in the writing of this book and who inspires me to expand my horizons, I give thanks for understanding all during the long process and for allowing my dream to become a reality.

Thanks to my mother, Nora Mae Hein, for the notes she made for me over the years. Much gratitude to my siblings, Dorothy McManners, LaVerne Chollett, Marie Isom Earls, Joyce Balke, Hugo Hein Jr., Lourene Falk, Virginia Asselin, and Sarah Muñoz, who provided me with their childhood memories to help Mom's story come to life. I am grateful to my deceased brother Henry Hein whose letters written to Mom frequently during his two-year army assignment aided my timeline. Thanks to my deceased brother Tilman Hein whose childhood bravery was recorded in the 1959 *Houston Chronicle* story "11-Year Old Till Has Kindness, Understanding Few of Us Get."

These special people were very helpful to answer my endless questions and help me track down phone numbers and information: Tinka Murray, Rev. Robert Tompkins, Cathy (Feick) Hutcheson, Rev. Virgil Pecht, Floy Mae Moravek, Linda (Law) Pinkerton, and Betsy (Neinast) Flencher.

I have compiled all the pieces to weave Mom's story. Special thanks to my sister Sarah who did the majority of the proofreading and to Joyce and Hugo who proofread small portions. Much appreciation flows to my sisters Lourene and Dorothy for the genealogical research they provided. I have diligently tried to keep the facts straight to give an accurate picture of Nora Mae Corley Hein. Should there be any errors that remain, they are unintentional and they are mine alone.

Alice

Chapter 1

My Earliest Memories

It was a tall white house in Garland, Texas. A house full of good times and laughter. Mama was there. Grandpa Schafer was there. Grandma Dora (my step grandmother) was there. But I can never remember Daddy being there. My little brother Charlie was there. Sometimes Aunt Lula was there. But I can't remember my Daddy ever being there – not ever.

I loved that house with its good times. We lived with my grandpa, Charlie Schafer, but Mama always said that we had to help earn our way. She was standing at the stove now, cooking some of her wonderful coconut candy. The candy was barely light brown in color as it cooked. I stood on a chair and leaned carefully to see into the pot. It looked so delicious! We dropped the fluffy white coconut in and stirred. When it reached perfection Mama spooned it onto wax paper to cool. When it was totally cooled, Mama wrapped the pieces in wax paper and put them in small paper bags. Today she saved a piece for me and a smaller one for Charlie who was only 2 years old. Charlie squealed with delight! I always helped Mama deliver the candy to the people in the neighborhood who had ordered it. She held Charlie's hand, or she carried him; and I carried the bags of candy. When we collected the money, I got to carry the money bag all the way home.

Mama and I both loved beautiful things. We had had our picture done once. I wore a lacey dress with a long waist. A satin ribbon was fastened around the waist. It looked like the ribbon was just tied in back, but actually it was stitched to the dress so it never came loose; even when I ran it stayed in place. This was my favorite dress! Mama had combed my hair to shine and put a beautiful bow on top of my head. I sat next to her on the short bench. She was all dressed up too. Mama was wearing a white dress that had a big white collar, I mean, a really large collar. The collar covered her entire shoulders with the lace on the edges extending beyond her shoulders. There were buttons in the front and Mama also had a colorful scarf wrapped around her middle section. The colors were bold and bright, but the picture was black and white so the scarf is barely noticeable, except to show off her small waist. This was a special picture for us; Mama wore her gold necklace which had a two inch cross in the front; she also wore a gold watch with a fancy band. The most noticeable thing is her lovely hat; it had a ribbon around it and a flower lying against the brim. We sat up straight for the photograph. We didn't particularly smile though. It wasn't considered proper to smile for a picture; it almost looked like I was frowning, but my heart was smiling. I just didn't like sitting still this long.

When we lived in the tall, white house I knew about a place called heaven. I had gotten a really pretty doll for Christmas. The doll was made of glass or porcelain; I am not sure which. I named her "Sallie." I accidentally dropped Sallie one day and she broke. I mean she really broke – there was a big crack across her forehead, but her entire nose and chin were in a jillion pieces. It was one of those "you can't fix it" moments. But I knew just what to do! I had a shoe box under the bed that I kept a few treasures in. I ran and emptied the shoe box. I carefully picked up all of the pieces of my doll and put them in.

"We can bury Sallie just like they did when Grandpa's brother's wife died," I thought. "Maybe she can go to heaven!" I knew about heaven because when we lived in the tall, white house we always went to Sunday School at a church near where we lived. Sunday School was where I had met friends and learned about God and Jesus and heaven. I took my little shoe box and went to find Grandpa Schafer.

"Can we bury Sallie, Grandpa?" I asked.

"What?" he mused, but seeing my sincere face he quickly added, "Sure." And so with a little help, I buried my pretty doll in the yard.

And Mama could create beautiful things! My mother, Nellie Mae Schafer Corley, made a lovely silhouette when she sat at the table with her back to the window. She was about five feet tall with strikingly black hair and brown eyes. Grandpa Schafer always said that I looked more like my daddy. I had honey blonde hair and soft blue eyes. With Mama's back to the window, the sun made a glow around her. I ran to sit next to her so I could watch more closely. Charlie stood next to Mama for about 15 seconds, then he played on the floor. He was not interested, but it seemed like magic to me! There was a single thread going in and beautiful lace coming out.

I watched intently as she held the shuttle she used with two fingers. The thread was attached and wound around the shuttle much like a bobbin. Mama would pull out a length of thread from the shuttle, wind that around the other hand, and pinch with the thumb and index finger. Then she would begin weaving it. She would slide the shuttle over the loop and flick the finger and then under the loop and flick the finger to pull it. She weaved over and under, over and under (or was it under, then over). Anyway, she did that twice to make a double stitch. After a certain number of stitches, somehow she pulled it to make a tiny ring. She called them "rings" and "chains."[1]

Mama said that the more even her stitches were the more beautiful the piece would be. She always worked slowly and carefully so her pieces were very lovely. Mama could make flowers, snowflakes, and butterflies! She said the end result all depended on how many rings and chains you put together as you connected them a certain way by using a different stitch called a "picot."[2]

Mama's mother, Annie Mary Schafer, had died when Mama was about six years old and Grandpa remarried the next year. Her stepmother Dora had taught her to make the lace. When I got a little older Mama was gonna' teach me to make lace. I so anticipated that day! For now, I could help by selling and delivering the lace she made and by being careful to bring home the money. People loved Mama's lace and someone always needed a gift for some occasion.

I was born on March 13, 1916, one year before World War I was declared (that was April 2, 1917) and one year before the 18th amendment "Prohibition" was passed (that was in December of 1917). I was born in Garland, Texas and was named Nora Mae Corley. For as long as I could remember Mama and I had lived with Grandpa Schafer. The onset of the 1920's saw a brief post war depression and then in 1922 a boom began which lasted until the stock market crash in 1929.[3] I was oblivious to all this history and things like the presidential election of 1928. My own life seemed to crash way before 1929.

The railroad industry had begun to suffer from the stiff competition of the trucking industry[3] and my Grandpa Schafer left his job at the railroad to become a custodian at a Dallas, Texas school before 1920. After Grandma Dora died (around 1921) Charlie and I had to accompany Mama when she helped Grandpa at the school. This presented a real challenge because in September, 1921 I was five years old and Charlie had just turned two. Needless to say, Mama was very distracted with Charlie and so the amount she could help was limited. Grandpa Schafer pondered what to do.

It was decided that Mama's younger sister, my Aunt Lula Schafer Hall, would come to live with us and help watch the kids so Mama could help Grandpa at the school in the evenings. Aunt Lula's husband Wallace would be away from home taking care of commitments for a while. Aunt Lula's coming to live with us was actually a help for her too.

After Grandma Dora died Grandpa Schafer became very sad. Ever since his job at the railroad had ended and he started working at the school things had become tighter. Mama was still selling her wonderful candy and as much lace as she could make, but it took a long time to make one beautiful piece of lace, and we kids were getting bigger and costing more. When I started school in the fall of 1922 I always had to use broken pencils. Grandpa saved the pencil pieces that he found on the school floor for me. It was one less thing to have to buy.

Grandpa devised a plan. When Uncle Wallace came home we would all move. Grandpa Schafer would sell his place and buy some farmland. We would move from the tall white house in Garland to Burleson County, Texas. Grandpa said that farming was in his blood. He was born in Ohio, the son of German-born farmers who later migrated to Texas and he knew farming well; but it had been a while since he had practiced it. Grandpa also said that moving to a farm would be better for the grandkids. After all, he wasn't getting any younger and we had to plan for the future.

So that's what we did. In the early spring of 1923, Grandpa sold his place and we started packing. When Uncle Wallace arrived home we loaded up. The tall white house seemed sad for us to go. The walls were now bare and the floor was swept. I went up and down the stairs several times. I paused and looked around slowly, drinking in my surroundings: the winding stairs, the tall windows with sunlight streaming in, the creaking door that Charlie and I sometimes hid behind when we teased Grandpa, the spot where I had stood watching Mama make lace. I didn't realize that I was leaving more than a house, I was leaving a part of me. Years later I was glad that I had lingered. I would never forget those memories.

"Come on, Nora Mae. We have to lock the door. We can't be late at the train station."

I twirled in the sunbeams once more. "Okay, Mama," I replied and ran out the door.

Chapter 2

Metamorphosis

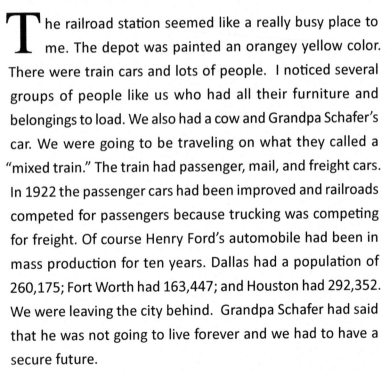

The railroad station seemed like a really busy place to me. The depot was painted an orangey yellow color. There were train cars and lots of people. I noticed several groups of people like us who had all their furniture and belongings to load. We also had a cow and Grandpa Schafer's car. We were going to be traveling on what they called a "mixed train." The train had passenger, mail, and freight cars. In 1922 the passenger cars had been improved and railroads competed for passengers because trucking was competing for freight. Of course Henry Ford's automobile had been in mass production for ten years. Dallas had a population of 260,175; Fort Worth had 163,447; and Houston had 292,352. We were leaving the city behind. Grandpa Schafer had said that he was not going to live forever and we had to have a secure future.

We boarded the train with great anticipation of what lay ahead. I loved climbing the train steps and holding the rail by myself. Mama had to hold onto Charlie, but I felt a bit of independence. We had six seats because there was Mama, Grandpa, Charlie, me, Aunt Lula and Uncle Wallace.

"Who wants to sit by the window?" Grandpa asked as he wiggled his glasses on his nose. His hair had been white and thin on top for as long as I could remember.

"I do! I do!" I exclaimed.

"Okay, Nora Mae. You take that seat." Mama sat with Charlie and I sat next to Grandpa Schafer. Mama was just glad to finally be on the train after all the time we waited in the depot while Grandpa and Uncle Wallace made sure all of our stuff was loaded.

When the conductor shouted "All Aboard," it was none too soon for us. The train began rolling. I waved to the people standing at the train station. I enjoyed watching the buildings of the city as they began to fly past my window. After what seemed a long time we left the city behind and I gazed intently at the countryside. I watched the land and trees, eagerly anticipating the houses that were scattered along the way. We continued for several hours.

As we passed through Waco the engineer received a message that a rainstorm which had preceded us to the area had flooded the track farther south. By the time we approached the small community of Reagan, Texas a safety plan had been devised. The train screeched to a halt. I could see puffs of smoke caused by the brakes forcing the wheels to slide against the tracks. We had no choice.

The conductor bellowed, "Please stay seated. The railroad tracks are under water. We will spend the night here which will allow time for the water to recede from the tracks." Everyone was stunned. No one had planned to spend the night on the train. Our trip was to be several hours, yes. But no overnight provisions had been made. The Pullman railroad cars of the time had fancy sleep cars, but this route needed none of those. This train ran from Dallas to Fort Worth to Houston. The return trip was Houston to Fort Worth to Dallas. There were many small town stops in between.

This day we were stuck at Reagan, Texas. We had no choice. There was food to buy, but that would only add to this already expensive trip. Grandpa and Mama made sure we kids ate something. Grandpa Schafer even milked the cow so Charlie could have milk to drink. Aunt Lula and Uncle Wallace tried to cheer us up. All of the passengers slept on the train. My wonderful adventure seemed temporarily like a stuffy mess. But I hoped for a "sunny day tomorrow," and was not disappointed!

We were able to get rolling the next morning. It was a bit frightening as the train took us through the flooded area. Looking out my window I saw water everywhere. I looked across the train and could see water out the other window also. It appeared that we were roaring on the water. I didn't close my eyes, but I was thankful when land appeared. By that evening we had arrived safely at our destination, gotten off the train, reloaded all of our stuff, and proceeded to our new home: Grandpa's new farm.

My! We were in the woods! We had passed neighbors as we drove in, but none were really close. Seeing the new place gave me a shot of energy, just thinking of a "new home!" The adults were dog-tired and, of course, this was not a "new home," just new to us. We unpacked nothing but our blankets that evening. We all slept on the blankets on the floor.

The next day Grandpa Schafer and Uncle Wallace unloaded all the stuff. Mama and Aunt Lula got our things situated in the new place. We now lived in a small farming community called Birdsong. Grandpa was in a rush to get the crops going. There was so much to do. I was very excited when they enrolled me in the school at Birdsong. It was a one room school having one teacher who taught all grades. This was so not like the school I had attended in Garland. Nonetheless, there was plenty to learn and I was intrigued.

Grandpa Schafer and Uncle Wallace soon made friends with the neighboring farmers. Grandpa needed tips about the local growing season, what crops did best, where to get seeds, and how to proceed. He also had to borrow a few items. He struck up a friendship really quickly with a neighboring farmer named Mr. Brinkmann. Brinkmann was an experienced farmer and he was of German ancestry just like Grandpa. This community seemed perfect for us. There were numerous people of German and Czechoslovakian descent. Before World War I many of the German Americans often sympathized with the Central Powers (Germany, Turkey, and Austria-Hungary).[3] The United States under President Woodrow Wilson had tried to remain neutral, but Germany's threat to sink all ships – passenger or merchant- had forced us to join the Allies (England, France, and Russia) in the fight. The realities of the war had changed the German American attitudes, but now many of them resented the Prohibition law.

Mr. Brinkmann was not generally a friendly man, but he and Grandpa Schafer sort of needed each other's assets. Grandpa really needed the advice of a successful farmer. Mr. Brinkmann who was a widower having five children, needed a wife and Grandpa had an available daughter. As fate would have it Mama did marry him in July of 1923. The two men had discussed it at length. Brinkmann had agreed that if he could marry Mama he would allow her to continue washing clothes and cooking for Grandpa. Charlie and I had to pack our things and move away from Grandpa Schafer. And now, here we were.

The reality was that Mama had married an old man! Brinkmann was 41 years old and Mama was 26. Plus, this old man had five children. All of the children were older than I was. I had met them at school, but they had never come to play. Actually, it was not uncommon for widowers of the day to marry younger women. Many wives died because of the hard work or from complications of childbirth, but this was a completely different way of life than I had known. I now lived on an active farm and all we knew was work, work, work. I had known love and happiness. This was the beginning of the years that seem like a nightmare, or a bad dream to me.

This life on a farm was so, so different. With all the people in our household, I am not sure how I began to feel very alone. It seemed that my new siblings didn't really want a new mother, let alone new kids in the house. It was a fact that we never went to church. The only <u>Bible</u> that the "Old Man" had was kept locked away in a trunk with important papers tucked away in it. I knew about Jesus, but never knew him in a personal way. We were not allowed to go play with neighboring children, not even on Sundays. We never went to church and we weren't permitted to read that locked up <u>Bible</u>. I missed going to Sunday School and church and I really missed having friends.

By 1926 my hair was cut short like the rest of the Brinkmann girls. Bobbed hair for girls was a style of the 1920's, but these cuts were also convenient for farm life. We had no time for frivolous things like fixing one's hair.

The first day of school was always a happy day for me. I wished school would never end. I discovered that math was easy for me. I could hardly wait for time for math lessons. When the younger students were supposed to be doing their practice sets, I would always focus on the teacher's lesson for the higher grades. Most of the time I could get the answer before the older students did, but I never told anyone. I just always did the problems silently and felt great inner satisfaction knowing that none of the math was too hard for me. Math was like music to me. I loved school and I studied to make good grades. School was my only escape from home which now seemed to me more like a prison than a home. I learned to hate it.

Have you ever felt like you weren't wanted? Have you ever felt like you were being blamed for everything that went wrong? That's how I felt. The good things that I did went unnoticed or someone else was given credit for them – always. Mama never seemed to care for me. She was always taking care of the other kids and trying to please the "Old Man."

Our family kept growing. In May of 1924 Mama had a baby girl. In May of 1926 she had another baby girl. I had three stepsisters, two stepbrothers, one brother (Charlie), and now two half-sisters. My stepbrothers didn't seem to want Mama, Charlie, and I there. When we kids were together, one of them always called Mama a "bitch." This was never to her face, of course, just to my face. I always thought of their dad as the "Old Man." I never said it to his face either, of course.

The "Old Man" never disciplined the boys for their mean-ness towards me. Their mother had been dead a long while and they were used to answering to their daddy only, or just doing what they wanted. They more than resented us. At first it was just small pranks, but then one of the boys threw a wrench at me, missing only by an inch! I thought that the

"Old Man" saw it, but he never corrected him. In May of 1928 Mama had a baby boy. I was now twelve years old and doing much of Mama's work.

We went to a county fair once. A <u>Bible</u> company was throwing out little <u>Bibles</u> and little books from the <u>Bible</u>. I got a book called <u>The Gospel of St. John</u>. I had to hide to even read it because it wasn't allowed. If the moon was full I would sneak the book with me outside and read on the way to the outhouse. Sometimes I hid behind the barn. The only time we went to church was when a new baby came along. It was a celebration of sorts. We would go to church so the baby could be baptized (sprinkled); then we would have a big dinner; then we would all go back to our farm work. I might have gone to church three or four times during those eight years. Can you even imagine that? I was so lonely.

And Grandpa Schafer was struggling with this new life too. After Mama got married, Brinkmann wouldn't let her help Grandpa anymore. Mama wouldn't of had time anyway, having inherited five children ages 16, 13, 11, 9, and 8. All of this responsibility was in addition to me and Charlie. But still, it was a blow to Grandpa. It turned out that he had picked a really bad time to go back to farming. Few people saw the Stock Market Crash and the Great Depression coming. The entire population would eventually be affected. These were the years just prior to that.

When cheerful Aunt Lula and Uncle Wallace decided to move back to Dallas County, Grandpa just couldn't do it anymore. The farm was too much responsibility for one person. Grandpa was ruined financially. He lost everything and returned to Garland himself. By 1929 per capita farm income in the United States was $273 compared to the national average per capita income of $681.[3] 1929 was bad for everyone, but especially for farmers. There were rivers of tears shed by me when Grandpa Schafer left. As he hugged me goodbye, he whispered in my ear,

"Nora Mae, if you ever want to find your father, I can help you do that. Take good care of yourself."

Grandpa could see the nightmare that I was living in. My "bright future" was looking pretty bleak.

School was the only place for me to see friends. The last day of school was always a crying day for me. I was never permitted to go anywhere else. I was not allowed to go to the neighbors to play. I was never allowed to go to town. Why did it have to be such a prison? After one of the children purposefully chopped me in the head with a hoe and received no punishment, I began to feel afraid. Not even Mama spoke up for me. It seemed that the bond between Charlie and I remained strong. They made fun of him, but I was the one that felt abused.

When the barn caught on fire, I was the one who was blamed for it. I wasn't even near the barn and I was pretty sure it was one of the boys smoking cigarettes in there that started the fire, but I was whipped severely. In May of 1930 Mama had another baby girl and I finished seventh grade.

When I was told that I had to quit school to work on the farm all the time, it literally seemed like I couldn't breathe. I was so tired of it all.

I put the few clothes that I had in a cloth flour sack, not a paper bag that might make noise. When everyone was asleep and the house seemed eerily quiet, I went down the stairs and out into the night. I was so afraid that the dog would bark and give me away, but he didn't. I held my breath as I crossed the yard. I did not look back once. I kept walking in the dark until I came to the home of some neighbors in our community.

John and Matilda Faust allowed me to stay with them. My family never did bother to come try to find me or anything. I took care of the Faust's son who was about two years old. I cleaned house, worked in the field, and did anything I could to earn my stay. The Fausts allowed me to go to Sunday School on Sundays with other neighbor girls. We had such fun just chatting as we walked the two miles or so to the church and back.

It was a daring move, but I did it! I located my father through Grandpa Schafer. My father said that he would send money for me to come visit him. After a long wait, the money arrived, and I boarded the train with enthusiasm. I was fourteen years old and I had lots of hope fluttering in my heart. I was going to meet my daddy for what was essentially the first time. I was a baby the last time we had seen each other. What would he be like?

Would he like me?

In the letter he sounded nice, but……

Stop it! He had responded to me, hadn't he? I let hope settle in my heart.

Here I was on a train again, rushing toward my future.

Chapter 3

Teenage Years

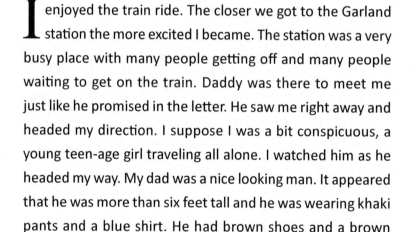

I enjoyed the train ride. The closer we got to the Garland station the more excited I became. The station was a very busy place with many people getting off and many people waiting to get on the train. Daddy was there to meet me just like he promised in the letter. He saw me right away and headed my direction. I suppose I was a bit conspicuous, a young teen-age girl traveling all alone. I watched him as he headed my way. My dad was a nice looking man. It appeared that he was more than six feet tall and he was wearing khaki pants and a blue shirt. He had brown shoes and a brown belt. He walked briskly, confidently I'd say. As he approached I could see that his hair was dark honey blonde with lots of platinum gray above the ears and his eyes were soft blue, like mine. He flashed a big grin.

"Nora Mae?" he asked.

"Yes. Daddy?" My heart seemed to jump into my throat.

He put his hands on my shoulders.

"My, you are all grown up." He hugged me and then I saw tears in his eyes. "It has been a really long time. I have thought of you often. I am your father, Ruel Corley."

I almost felt guilty. I had thought of him off and on over the years, but not often. Well, not often, that is, until the last few months. He had seemed almost like a mirage or like a fictional story, not real.

"Come on. I want you to meet my family. Let me have your bag." I was thankful that I had managed to borrow a decent looking suitcase for the trip. It was sort of small, but I didn't need much.

He took the bag. I hadn't even thought about him having a family. I wasn't surprised. I just hadn't thought about it. We walked inside the depot and toward a group of people seated in the larger waiting room. There were always two waiting rooms in those days – one for "coloreds" and the other for the rest of the population. I could see that the group was actually a woman and seven children. Daddy set down my bag.

"I want you to meet……my wife Lillian." Lillian stood up. She was a bit taller than me, but not much and she had reddish hair and a soft smile. "And these are our children." He continued, "John Pershing is thirteen years old. Sarah is ten. Henry Roland is nine." Daddy paused as he introduced each one. "Ruel Junior is eight. Anne Louise is six. Grace is four. The baby is Dorothy. She is two."

Dorothy liked me immediately. She put out her arms for me to take her, so I did. She was so cute with her curls.

"Nice to meet you all," I said.

There was an awkward pause and then Daddy introduced me. "I would like all of you to meet Nora Mae. She is my daughter."

"Who?" Lillian asked.

He repeated, "My daughter, Nora Mae."

I started to smile, but Lillian's face was turning ashen. She gasped and ran away from us, down the hall, and then into the Ladies Restroom. Daddy ran right behind her.

I stood frozen, Dorothy still in my arms.

"Are you really his daughter?" One of the boys asked.

"Yes. I am," I stammered.

"And how old are you? Where did you come from?" he continued. The questions seemed to pour from him, but his attitude was simply inquisitive, not rude.

I explained to them that I was born in Garland and that we had moved away when I was six years old.

"Are we your brothers and sisters?" one of the girls asked.

Sarah laughed. She had bright red hair and was thin. "We have to be, sort of, I guess."

I knew all about stepbrothers, stepsisters, half-brothers and the like. I understood it perfectly. I guess I was a pro.

I spelled it out, "You are my half-brothers and half-sisters because we have the same father, but not the same mother. I actually have three more half-sisters, one more half-brother, three stepsisters, two stepbrothers, and one brother!"

"Wow! How many is that?"

"I've never even counted it all yet. I just heard about you all today. Let's see. If I count..."

Ruel Junior interjected, "We just now heard about you too. We thought we were just riding along with daddy to pick up his check. He works for the Cotton Belt Railroad."

"If I count all the girls," I began again, "I have four, plus three, plus three more, so that's ten sisters. And then I have three brothers, plus two, plus one, plus one more. That's seven brothers. So I guess I have seventeen brothers and sisters."

"Actually we had one more brother. It was Anne's twin, Andrew. He died when he was a baby. So you really have eighteen brothers and sisters! Wow! That's a lot!"

"You're not kidding," I thought to myself.

By now Daddy and Lillian were coming walking back. Whatever he explained to her about me he told her in the bathroom, so I didn't get to hear. I could tell she had been crying, but she extended her hand to me.

"Hello, Nora Mae. It is Nora Mae, right? I am your step-mother, Lillian."

We headed "home." There was so much conversation among all the kids that I forgot the awkwardness for a few days.

While at my daddy's I learned all kinds of things about myself. I learned things about my genealogy. All of a sudden my Corley grandparents were "real people." I saw pictures of them. I even heard stories that I may be kin to Daniel Boone because my daddy was born in Tennessee and his mother was Sarah Elizabeth "Sallie" (or was it "Sally" – I wish I had written it down) Boone who was born in Lebanon, Tennessee in 1862. Grandma and Grandpa had married in Tennessee and then migrated to Texas in 1910.

Another interesting, but sad thing was that my Grandpa, William Daniel "Buck" Corley, was one of fifteen people killed in the Garland Cyclone, a tornado occurring on May 9, 1927. That was three years ago. Both of my grandparents were blown sixty yards by the cyclone. A house belonging to a man named Ben Alexander had been blown a block away from its foundation. The entire house had been transported by the winds. Grandma was found alive inside the house. Saws and axes were used to rescue Grandpa from under the house, but he died that same day. A newspaper clipping dated May 10, 1927 confirmed the story. The paper was the *Dallas Morning News*. I also learned that one of my ancestors was in the Revolutionary War.

I saw pictures of my daddy when he was young. Daddy was more than six feet tall and he had been this really good looking young guy.

Meeting my daddy and learning about my family seemed to give me a new strength within my personality.

A week or so passed. I saw the routine of their family life. I learned that Daddy's job at the railroad took him away a lot. I began to have that same old lonely feeling.

"You are really something, Nora Mae," I told myself. "You have more siblings than anyone you know and you still manage to feel lonely."

But another thing was that because I had had so much responsibility for such a long time I found it impossible to fit in as a child. I was grown, well practically grown.

Daddy was sad when I told him that I had decided to return to the people that I had been staying with. He took me to the train station the next day. When he hugged me goodbye he said, "We'll stay in touch. I'll be coming to visit so always let me know where you are."

I was surprised. Daddy did care about me.

I returned to my "home" a bit disillusioned, but more focused. I could see my path a little more clearly. I had this tremendous hope within me even though my path seemed very limited. I am not sure where the hope I had originated. This was 1930 and the entire nation was struggling. I lived with the Fausts for over a year. Then I lived with Mrs. Barton and her daughter Louise Urbanosky. They were more into the social scene and I met a lot of people while I lived there.

Early in 1932 I met a young man named Pete Hein. Pete was well mannered and polite and he was interested in me. If Pete knew that I would be at a certain place, he would show up there.

On my sixteenth birthday, which was March 13, I met his older brother Hugo. Mrs. Barton sent me to borrow a chicken to set on some eggs. As I walked back carrying the hen (that was a trip), I noticed a man working on the neighbor's fence. He smiled and joked about the hen. We introduced ourselves as I walked on. He called after me. I saw him again soon after.

Hugo's flamboyant personality captured my heart. He could make me laugh. He could make everyone laugh. How long it had been since I had really felt like laughing, I couldn't remember. Hugo had a knack for telling stories. His father, William Carl Hein, was a farmer in our area, another German farmer. Mr. Hein was also a blacksmith. He had a blacksmith shop on the farm and he fixed plows and other tools for the neighbors. He also made horseshoes.

Hugo talked about how his dad had purchased a steel bellows, which was a blower used for the coals, when Hugo was just a kid. Hugo and his brother Pete had had the job of turning the blower to keep the coals hot as their daddy worked. Hugo said they would get bored and would start turning it faster and faster until everything would be red hot. Hugo would laugh as he told how his dad would exclaim, "Boy, you're burning it up! Slow it down! Slow it down!"

He would mimic his father's German accent as he told the story. Mr. Hein had grown up speaking German, later learning English, and his wife Mary Anna Dungen Hein had taught him to read English. Hugo had learned German as a child and I giggled to hear him use phrases like "My shoe went kaputt" or "Don't forget to outen the light." I loved the German words. They were in my roots too. How he changed "ausschalten" to "outen" was clever.

Hugo poked fun at Pete. He told this story. On one occasion when Pete had done something wrong, Mr. Hein called him down the next morning. There was a wooden water barrel on the porch and the procedure was that any offender had to bend over that barrel and receive a whipping with a rope. Knowing this, Pete grabbed a coat and stuffed it in the back of his pants as he headed toward the stairs. His idea was to soften the blow.

Pete was unaware that he had a hole in the back of his pants. As he ran toward the stairs, one of the coat sleeves was dangling from the hole. His brothers snickered because they saw it as he ran out. There was not time to warn him. Their daddy who was waiting at the bottom of the stairs saw it too. He grabbed the sleeve. "What you got there, boy?" He pulled it all out and Pete got more than was planned. Everyone could hardly stop laughing when Hugo would tell about that coat sleeve dangling.

Yes. My heart was definitely captured.

There was a community dance coming up and as the group talked about it, I overheard Pete say, "If Hugo's gonna' be there, I may as well not go." Hugo who was 26 years old was as taken with me as I was with him. When he proposed marriage, I accepted immediately. I so wanted to have a home of my own.

Less than one month from the day we met, we married. The date was April 11, 1932. Hugo's sister Bessie Hein and Henry Draehm got married the same day. Reverend A.S. Broaddus performed the double wedding ceremony at his home in Caldwell, Texas. Rev. Broaddus worked at Simpson's Grocery Store and he took an hour off from work to come home and marry us. I had shopped and found the perfect dress. It was my size; it was beautiful, a dream come true! But then.....I saw the price tag. I quickly put it back and chose another one. Not because I liked it, but because I had enough money to pay for it.

Being only sixteen, I had to make a false statement to get a marriage license. The lady didn't question me. I had always looked older than I was. Charlie Orsak and Gerlina Thuber stood as our witnesses. Albert Schrader and Lillie Duncan stood for Henry and Bessie. We meant those vows.

I later went to visit Mama to let her know that I was now married. The "Old Man" went out the back door and stayed outside while we visited. I told Charlie all about how I had gone to meet Daddy and how we had a "zillion" half-brothers and half-sisters. I described each one. And I told him that Daddy had promised to visit me. "I will let you know when he comes." It felt good to be in touch with Mama again.

The economy was depressed. We moved into Hugo's parents' rent house. We lived on a farm and we tried to be farmers. We worked with a yoke of oxen. We both worked hard. The whole nation was in a slump. In our area people began to call armadillos "Hoover hogs" because so many folks had to eat them. We desperately needed something.

Franklin D. Roosevelt gave a radio address before the election that fall. In his radio address he outlined a program that he wanted to build for the average American, whom he called the "forgotten man." At the Democratic National Convention he spoke about his New Deal which was to use government funds to build schoolhouses, streets, roads, and bridges. Other useful tasks like cleaning up parks were to become job opportunities also.

Many folks felt forgotten and identified with FDR. He won the election in November. Hugo grubbed stumps for $ 0.75 a day to buy fruit for our first Christmas.

Someone gave me a copy of the New Testament and I began to read it. I knew that I needed more of God in my life, but I didn't know what to do. I did feel that I needed to go to church. I still had those great memories from my childhood: God, Jesus, heaven. I wanted to go to church, but Hugo didn't see the need. So we only went once in a while.

On January 6, 1933 our first baby arrived. The baby was so large that I had difficulty giving birth. The midwife Lizzie Gracy tried everything she knew to do. I finally had the baby while standing up with Hugo and Lizzie holding me up. It was a ten pound girl and she was beautiful. We named her Dorothy Lee. In spite of the trauma of her birth, she was spunky. Our family rejoiced, but there were the nagging comments, "Not a boy to work on the farm."

In March of 1933, President Roosevelt began implementing his promises. He created the CWA (Civil Works Administration) and the CCC (Civilian Conservation Corps) to get jobs going. He also fulfilled a promise he had made to repeal Prohibition. I had never envisioned that it would be legal to sell alcoholic beverages. I wasn't blind, I knew about moonshine, but Prohibition had been the law since I was one year old. I never imagined that I would have to deal with it.

Chapter 4

A Prayer and a Promise

I was now settling into my routines as a wife and mother. The farm kept me busy. The price for crops continued to drop lower, but at least we had some food crops. The dreadful "alcohol for sale" began to affect us because Hugo was affected greatly when he drank it. We had a lot of ups and downs.

When Daddy wrote to say that he was coming for a visit we were excited. Hugo rode over to tell my brother, Charlie Corley. Charlie was now fourteen years old. He was getting taller, just like Daddy, but his hair was very dark and his eyes were brown like Mama's. He had dimples when he smiled. We all expected that Daddy would visit Charlie too. "Old Man" Brinkmann bought Charlie new overalls, anticipating the visit. When Daddy just stayed at our house during the entire visit, Hugo asked him point blank, "Are you Charlie's father?"

"No," Daddy replied.

"No? Well who in the tarnation is his father?"

"I don't know," Daddy said. "Nellie Mae and I divorced before Nora Mae was a year old. I honestly do not know."

I was shocked. I'd always assumed that I had at least one "true" sibling. It seemed that Charlie and I had always been together. Now I began to weep as Daddy spoke. I wept for Charlie who was waiting with the new overalls, waiting for nothing. Who was his father? I wept for Mama who had endured so much. Now that I had full responsibility for one child, I could see her huge responsibility more clearly – eleven children to help raise! I couldn't imagine such a thing. I wondered if Mama could even find her lace-making shuttle these days.

July 14, 1934 was Hugo's twenty-ninth birthday. His father unexpectedly died that day. Hugo now needed a son more than ever if we hoped to be successful on the farm. In November of 1934 our second baby arrived. We named the beautiful, bouncing girl, LaVerne. I was excited just thinking about two girls to be best friends. Anticipation among our friends had been high. Again I heard the, "not a boy, not a boy" comment. "We will hope for next time."

In 1936 we moved to the New Tabor Community. Our closest neighbors, Paul and Lillie Faust, lived about a half mile away. They didn't have any children so they enjoyed our girls tremendously. When the weather would get bad, they would come and spend the night with us. On July 4th the rain pounded, but Paul went to Deanville to the annual barbecue which was a big celebration. Lillie came to spend the night with us. It was just getting dark when I realized that I was going into labor.

Hugo galloped about a mile on horseback to borrow a phone so he could call the doctor. On his way back he could hear the "put put" engine sounds of the doctor's car coming from the opposite direction. Suddenly there was a loud crashing noise and then the "put put" died out. Hugo immediately went to check it out. The doctor had run off the narrow bridge with his front wheel. Dr. Goodnight was frustrated, but he refused to ride on the horse. So he walked the rest of the way, with Hugo carrying his bags on the horse. Our third child, made her grand entrance a little after midnight, a July 5th girl.

My heart was now softening toward Mama. We named our adorable baby Nellene Marie . "Nellene" was for Mama (Nellie Mae) and "Marie" was for Hugo's mother, Mary. Dr. Goodnight slept on our porch the remainder of the night. The next morning Hugo went and got Paul Faust to come with his mules and wagon. They drove the wagon to the creek, and with the help of the mules, they rescued the doctor's car which was hanging off the bridge. What a rainy mess!

In a few days, Hugo's sister Irene came and stayed with us to help with the work. With three little girls, there was so much to do. Irene was such a blessing to us. A few weeks later, a couple of Hugo's friends came and stayed an entire week with us. This made things harder; they definitely were not helping out. We didn't have enough food for us, let alone for two more adult men.

I don't know how we got behind. It seemed like we must have started out behind. It was the same old story – no food, no job. We couldn't catch up.

I began to realize the situation we were in. All around people struggled and we were in the middle of the Depression, but Hugo's lack of education affected us too. I had heard the story many times. It remains one of the saddest stories I have ever heard. When Hugo was in the fourth grade he and his cousin decided to skip school. They fished a little, talked and laughed, and goofed off the entire day.

Someone snitched and when the word got to Mr. Hein, he dealt the punishment. He had quite a bit of land that he needed to clear and he was needing help, so he said to them, "Boys, if you do not want to go to school, you do not have to go to school. From now on, when the other kids go to school you two will stay and work with me on the farm." And that was that! Hugo had to quit school in fourth grade. There was no protest, no visit from the school truant officer, and there was no curriculum for home schoolers. The year was 1915 and Hugo was 9 years old. His cousin was about the same age. All their schooling from here on was to be in the "school of hard knocks." Gosh – they were so young to be in that school already.

Mr. Hein who farmed cotton and corn assumed that his boys would grow up to be farmers. He didn't see the need for much education. If one could read, write, and count their money, that was enough. He had six sons and five daughters; they all began working on the farm at an early age. For recreation they had fishing, hunting, and swimming. Some of the younger siblings did graduate from high school. Mr. Hein had no way of knowing that our country was moving away from agriculture and that because of this, one's education would become more and more important.

I saw the situation we were in: three small children, no food, and no job. It was so overwhelming. I didn't know what to do. The crops were finished for the year. I had no transportation if I wanted to work; and we lived in the country. My cupboard was bare. We needed food, toiletries, everything. Dorothy and LaVerne were napping so peacefully, so trusting, so unaware that I had no food for the next meal. I grabbed the baby (Nell) and ran out to the barn. I placed her on the last bit of hay and kneeling there, I cried out to God, whoever He was and wherever He was.

"God, I know that you're out there, but it seems that I can't find you. Please hear me! Help us provide food and shelter for the children you have given us."

I picked up the baby, and lifting her high I continued, "Oh, God who has ears to hear me, please hear me. I dedicate this child to you. Show me how to teach my kids about you. I will teach them about you. Amen." I wiped away my tears, adjusted the blanket on Nell, and hurried back to the house.

Shortly, Hugo's brother Joe came by, bringing us a sack full of black-eyed peas! Hope again swelled up inside of me. God had answered my prayer! Hugo and a man (I wish I could recall his name) went fishing and killed bullfrogs for us to eat. So we made it through that desperate fall and winter. The next year we had to borrow money from Hugo's mother to pay our bills. We had a few chicken and eggs and we milked one of the landlord's cows. I cooked lots of cornbread and fried cornmeal cakes. By the end of the year it was evident that we couldn't repay the money we had borrowed. Hugo's mother had given us some land that she had hoped would help us get started on Hugo's dream of farming. We gave the land back to her to repay the money we owed. In January of 1938, we transferred the deed back to her, but we did retain our mineral rights. Our hearts were so sad, but at least one debt was paid.

We had to move again. This time we moved to the Harmony Community to C.C. Martin's place. In March of 1938 Helen Joyce was born. Lizzie Gracy was the midwife who delivered her. Lizzie did really well and my heart delighted in my beautiful, healthy little girl. The comments were louder now, "Another girl?" "Another girl!" "Is that four girls?" "My! My!"

In late March the air turned cold and everything froze. The corn we had struggled to get planted froze, but it came out again later! We had two cows to milk so now we had plenty of milk and butter. When Hugo wasn't working he picked berries. I canned 128 quarts of dewberries. They were so good! It had been a long while since we had eaten our hearts desire of fruit. We planted a garden too. I canned everything I could can from the garden.

On the national scene, the CWA was short-lived. It appeared that the laws passed to end the Depression weren't working. Other programs were created to try to provide jobs for the large number of unemployed folks. The PWA (Public Works Administration) and the WPA (Works Progress Administration) were created. Highway 36 was being built through Burleson County as one of those projects. Hugo got a job and worked there some. Things looked a little better for a short while.

Hobos, or jobless beggars, were seen frequently. It was sort of ironic that we who had the least income and the most mouths to feed were the ones that many hobos were attracted to. Maybe it was the sounds of children playing that attracted them to our house. Or it could have been that we often lived along the route that was becoming Highway 36. It was a major route connecting central Texas to Houston.

Sometimes the hobos were people that Hugo had met previously who were now down on their luck. We turned very few away. I got really good at adding water to the peas, water to the gravy, water to the corncakes, water to whatever, and stretching the meal. One meal for a hobo was okay with me, but if they tried to stay longer they had to help out somehow.

The kids learned to watch the cup or glass used by the hobo. They would refuse to drink from that cup or glass later. I had had it with them arguing over who had to drink out of "that" cup so I named one of the glasses the "hobo glass" and no one else ever drank out of it. I always tried to treat the hobos with dignity and respect even though many were dirty and unkept. (Hobos sought us out as late as the 1950's.)

In 1939 we had to move again. All this moving! How I longed for a place that we could call our own, but I could do nothing about it. We were lucky we had a roof over our heads. This time we moved to Aunt Minnie Schumacher's rental place. It was in the middle of the cotton patch. I guess we were tenant farmers. We didn't own the land, but we helped farm it. We usually did some type of work to pay for our rent.

State brochures in later years wrote about people like us – stating that tenant farmers were the most serious social issue faced by the state of Texas at the time.[4] We didn't know we were a "social issue." We thought we were intelligent people just doing what we had to do to make it. I guess we were sort of clawing our way to survival.

Chapter 5

Unstable Employment

Dorothy started school at High Prairie School in September of 1939. Just thinking about all the things that she would learn made me excited for her. It was decided that the teacher, Mr. Steve Schiller, would pick up Dorothy and the Gaas girls (our neighbors) and give them a ride to school. I made sure she had what she needed for school. It was important to me that she start school with good pencils, not small broken ones like I had on my first day of school. I was enthusiastic, but a tiny bit apprehensive to see her off that first day. My first child was starting school!

The birth of our fifth child on September 20th was a joyous occasion. Lizzie Gracy was again the assisting midwife. When "he" arrived, that's right, "he," Hugo proudly announced, "It's a boy!" The German American farmers thought that maybe Hugo could become a true farmer after all. Now he had a boy to help out on the farm. But it was a bit late, we didn't even own property anymore so how could we be "real" farmers?

We named the baby Hugo Hein, Jr.; but I called him "Son." The German word was "Sohn." When I referred to my child, no one had to ask if the baby was a boy.

"Son was born just two weeks ago."

"Son rolled over yesterday."

"Son is sleeping six hours straight now."

"Son is sitting up on his own."

You get the idea.

While we lived on Aunt Minnie's place, Hugo's mother could walk to visit us. We lived about one fourth of a mile from her house. The girls would see her coming across the pasture and they would get excited. Grandma Hein always brought something when she walked over. The girls would watch the brown paper bag she would be carrying. If she gripped it with a fist, they knew she was bringing eggs, but if the top of the bag was folded over and down, she was bringing cookies! She made these wonderful little cookies that she called "tea cakes." We all loved them. If that brown bag appeared folded over at the top, the celebration would begin way before she arrived at the gate. Grandma Hein always knew the kids loved her.

One day when Son was almost two years old, he disappeared. I was frantic; I looked and looked and called his name. The girls helped search all the places he might be hiding, looking inside and outside. I finally saw him down in the pasture; the horses were circling him. Fear gripped my heart as I ran toward him with the four girls trailing behind me. As we got closer we could hear him crying. Son was crying loudly, but only because he was stuck in the grass burrs. He was not the least bit afraid of the horses. I began to pull the grass burrs from his clothes. He kept saying, "I want to go see Grandma. I want to go see Grandma." He was more than halfway to her house already.

When Son had been born I was 23 years old. I had been married for seven years. During that time I was either pregnant or carrying around a baby. Sometimes I was pregnant and carrying around a baby. After seven years of marriage we had five children so I had been pregnant five times nine months which is forty-five months. I had thus far been pregnant a total of three years and nine months. All of the moving, planting, picking, working in the field was done with my kids around me. If I was in the cotton patch, the kids were too. When I was picking cotton, the youngest child would ride on top of my long cotton sack as I trudged along. The older girls had their own smaller sacks for picking and they would entertain the younger girls as we went along.

I had discovered a passion for sewing. Hugo had acquired a manual Singer sewing machine, the kind with the large pedal that you pump with your foot as you sew. The kids had to have clothes to wear so I made them. I was pretty good at sewing; it was easy for me to envision a pattern, draw it, cut it out, and pin it on.

For material I used the colorful cotton sacks that feed came in. Grandma Hein would save the feed sacks for me.

The feed store sold them really cheap and the material was really good. If I was careful to pull the threads just right, the seams would come apart with little or no damage to the material. Once I pinned my pattern to the material, it seemed that I was practically done. I sewed dresses for the girls, and shirts for Son. I could cut the dress pieces a little smaller for Nell and Joyce, or a little bigger for Dorothy and LaVerne. The feed sacks were brightly colored with patterns of flowers or some type of swirls in the print. The outfits were cute, not fancy, but cute.

People could tell that one's clothes were made of feed sacks because they would recognize the material patterns. Of course, no one worried about it, until they went to school and discovered that the whole world was not wearing feed sack clothes. A select few were actually buying their clothes.

Grandpa Schafer came to visit us every summer when he was on vacation from work and the kids looked forward to his visits. My daddy came to visit at various times. He always came alone, but he brought stories about the family and how everyone was growing up.

1940 greeted the cotton growers with a flood and the crops were ruined. The corn was ruined too. Hugo's brother, Raymond, and his wife Melinda left the farm and moved to Houston to find employment before the next planting season.

Hugo worked again on the WPA projects: construction of the Somerville High School football stadium and gymnasium and construction of the Caldwell High School gym. It was steady income for a short while, but that too ended. Hugo was now 34 years old. At age 26 years and 8 months, he had had no one to think of but himself and he could work for his father if all else failed. He would spend his free time with friends. Seven years later, he had a wife and five kids depending on him, his father was dead, and he had no job. None of his friends or siblings had as many mouths to feed as he did. Some of his old friends were still carefree.

If Hugo wanted to act carefree at times, he did. The big problem was the way that the wine he drank affected him. He would change from his calm, witty personality into a man of anger. I am not proud of this fact, but once he was so out of control and I was so afraid, that I grabbed a piece of firewood and hit him on the head. I learned that I could defend myself and that I could confidently tell the kids, "You don't have to be afraid." Drat that alcohol!

It was all too soon when we had to move again. Each time we moved it seemed like we had another kid and a few more things to pack and lug. This time we moved to the Krysteniks' place across from John Sablatura's store. It was a white house and it had four nice sized rooms, a hallway, two porches, and stunning yellow canna lilies off the south side of the house. There was an outside stairs going up to the attic. (No one would sleep up there). Two buildings, a garage, and a cotton barn were between the house and highway 36.

We were glad to be getting this house. We still wouldn't have electricity, but that was okay. None of our rural neighbors did either. History books record that two-thirds of Americans enjoyed electricity by the end of the 1920's. Lots of money was spent on vacuum cleaners, washing machines, refrigerators, and ranges. New appliances were easing the burdens of the housewives. Here it was 1940 and I still didn't even have electricity, certainly not electric appliances. But I did have a manual sewing machine, a wash tub with a decent rub board for washing clothes, five happy kids, and lots of hope for the future.

Soon we joined a church that was not too far away. We went as often as we could. I was very disappointed when I read about the Christians rejoicing in the <u>Bible</u>. Even after joining the church, I didn't seem to have the joy that the <u>Bible</u> spoke about. I wanted to cry, but who ever saw anyone cry in church? Something would be terribly wrong. My kids were happy kids and I was thankful, but I felt no joy in my spirit. The good thing was that I did have a lot of hope.

Hugo made an agreement with a man from Hearne, Texas. We would plant and grow a crop of peas. The man would come back when the peas were ready and pay us for them. He would pick them and take them to Houston to sell. We would make money and he would make money. We had to plant lots and lots of peas. Hugo was plowing the field and making the rows. The kids and I were planting. Dorothy and LaVerne had a big metal syrup bucket full of peas to plant.

They were so excited when they finally brought the empty bucket back to us. Of course we still had many more to plant. We filled the syrup bucket again; their little faces were so sad looking as they trudged back out to plant. Eventually they came back again. They said that they were done, and ran off quickly. Later, when the peas came up, I was surprised to see one spot with fifty or more seedlings all together. They had planted alright, but when they got tired, they must have dumped all the rest in one spot. (When the girls were older, they confessed to Alice, not to me, that they had dug what they thought was a deep hole on the farthest end of the row and dumped all the rest of the seed in.) Of course I was aggravated, but remembering their sad, little faces, I tried to help. I transplanted some of the seedlings and tossed others away so their daddy would not be able to see the full extent of what they had done.

It brought me so much contentment to hear the kids outside in the late afternoon, playing leap frog. I would remember it as I worked into the night, finishing up chores by candlelight or by coal oil lamp. My days were very long. Some evenings I collapsed in a heap as soon as the baby fell asleep. Thank God that there were no more hours in the days. I probably would have worn my body irreparably out.

Subconsciously I began to formulate a list of things that should be most important for raising children. These three things were my top priorities. These were the things I would fight for:

1) Sunday School – so they will know about God and also have some leisure times with friends
2) Public School – so they can learn important things about the world and about themselves; enough school so they can read and write and do the "best math ever" to count their money, figure their bills, and not get cheated; so they can meet a broader circle of friends
3) Parents who stay together to raise their children

Those were the three things that were most important to me. I would try to provide those three things for my children.

The kids were now going to Second Creek School. The schools were reorganizing their curriculum. Some students skipped a grade and they were expected to keep up. LaVerne had only finished first grade, but they put her in third grade. She cried every afternoon when she came home from school. After a few days of the flooding tears, I figured out that the other students had already learned to add and LaVerne was expected to do addition with two digit numbers when she had never been taught basic addition. I went to the school and asked them to please put her in second grade where she belonged. They did and once she was properly assigned, math became one of her best subjects. She seemed to have a head for numbers, just like me. Dorothy's curriculum gaps were not serious ones and she kept up with the older group with no problem.

It seemed to me that our wealth was destined to be only our children. They were all we had. If wealth was measured by counting the number of children families had, we were richer than most. However, when it came to providing for the kids, we were always struggling.

Hugo's grandmother, Mollie Dungen, died in August of 1941.

In December of 1941 the United States entered World War II. On January 1, 1942, our sixth child was born. We named him Henry Roland, after one of my half-brothers. The name sounded musical to me. We called him "Butch." Now we had two sons. Butch was a good baby, but with six kids, it seemed like there was more to do than ever.

The nation rallied around the war. "Also during this period, a number of Congressman came in to enlist in the Navy, including Former President Lyndon B. Johnson, who was the first member of Congress to go on active duty with the armed forces following the Pearl Harbor attack."[8] My half-brother Ruel Corley, Jr. was in the military. Hugo's brother Joe had 2 sons who went to war, Andrew and Jim. Hugo's brothers Pete and Leo joined the fight. Other cousins and neighbors went to war; everyone wanted to help out. Hugo volunteered to go, but was not accepted because he was 36 years old and had six children. He was very angry about the refusal. He worked on road maintenance for a while.

I was trying to keep all the household chores done, with the help of the kids, and milk the cows too. I fainted in the cow pen after I had finished milking the cow one day. Hugo was there; he poured the milk on my head and then he ran to a neighbor's house and called the doctor. I was just so run down. One day of rest and I had to be up and going again.

It wasn't long and I was diagnosed with tick fever. I battled it for months. A piece of flesh about ¾ inch by ½ inch rotted out of my right leg. It was on the right side of my knee.

When Hugo's road maintenance job played out, we were in a fix. The government was implementing rationing to insure fair distribution because of shortages in consumer goods caused by the war effort. We were short of a job. The bombing of Pearl Harbor had ignited fear. There were four million citizens of Germany, Italy, and Japan in the United States. One million one hundred thousand of those were quickly classified as "enemy aliens." Eventually eleven thousand Germans and German Americans would be interned in camps. At the beginning of the war some were detained and evicted from coastal areas. Hundreds were brought in from Latin America also.[5]

The war and the German prisoners were discussed at school. There was a fear overall. There were three internment camps in Texas which later became prison camps. The closest one to us was 150 miles away. It was rumored that there was a "secret" internment camp much closer to us. Some locals said that Hitler's brother was held in the "secret" camp. A preacher who owned a short wave radio to contact his relatives in Germany was suspected of being a spy. The rumors we heard may have been unfounded, but the fear we all felt was very real.

One rainy night we were awakened by three men jerking on the screen door, trying to come in. The screen doors were hooked, but it was frightening. All of the children were awakened by the noises: the rain, the banging door, the German chatter. Hugo cautiously went to the door. He could understand that they wanted to use the phone. He spoke to them in German, letting them know that we had no phone and no room. He instructed them to go across the road. He told them that maybe the neighbor could help them. They argued. They were cold and wet and wanted to come in, but he convinced them to leave. They did so. Their boots sounded loudly on the porch as they went off.

Afterwards we could not find Nellene. We looked for her, finally finding her hiding in the dirty clothes box that was in my closet. She was terrified and did not want to come out. The little curls on her forehead were damp.

"The German prisoners are here," she whispered. We assured her that the Germans were gone.

We all went back to bed and tried to sleep. There were lots of little bodies in our bed the rest of the night. We later learned that the neighbor had allowed the three Germans to stay in his barn, out of the rain. The next morning his daughter caught the bus to Caldwell where she worked, as was her routine. Her husband had gone to war so she and her child had come home to be with her parents. Arriving in Caldwell, she went to the sheriff before she proceeded to work. The sheriff went and got the three men out of the barn. It was believed that these were Germans who had escaped one of the internment camps.

By August of 1942 I was pregnant again. Hugo was without a job. Crops were finishing. The WPA which had begun in 1935 was being phased out by the government. There was no hope of a job there. We were on the verge of desperate – again.

Chapter 6

Resolve Leads to ... the Cotton Patch

H ugo was not the only one who struggled to find employment. I tried to think of ways to help out. It was suggested to me that we give the children away.

"No." I said it emphatically. But they continued. They explained that it had been done before; there was no shame in it. The children grew up in good homes being well cared for. The parents had contentment because they knew that they had done the best thing for their children.

"There are plenty of people around who have no children." That was a true statement. Even some of Hugo's brothers had no children.

"No," was all I could say. I suddenly felt very weak. I could never choose some kids to "give away" and some "to keep." It sounded crazy to me. I was more determined than ever that we would survive. My kids were my treasures; my heart was wrapped around each one equally.

"Just think about it at least. Your kids are good kids and people will want them…"

"No," I repeated. The determination within me swelled almost to anger. "We may all have to work to make it, but we will make it!"

I began to do chores for hire within the community. People paid me to sew for them or wash and iron for them. I even did quilting. My kids helped with our chores at home and also helped by watching the little ones while I did other people's chores for income. Hugo did a lot of handyman jobs.

In May of 1943 Lourene Louise was born, another beautiful girl. I was simply amazed that I now had seven children. I was continually haunted by the prayer I had prayed in the barn seven years ago. I had promised to teach the kids about God. My kids were not the only ones who did not get to go to Sunday School very often, but it bothered me enormously.

I talked to the pastor. Rev. Modschiedler agreed that he and Mrs. Leona Poppe would do a Vacation Bible School at my house. The VBS was successful and so they started having "Sunday" School at my house every Saturday. We used the big room that was next to the kitchen as the classroom. We invited other kids who lived in the country community; as many as twenty youngsters came to the classes. I loved the sounds of laughter and enjoyed the <u>Bible</u> lessons as much as the kids did. (The Saturday "Sunday" School would continue at our house for three years.)

Our corn crop did really well and I canned 48 quarts of corn for our pantry. John and Erma Lacina brought their corn over. They helped prepare it for canning. We had to shuck it, cut the kernels off the cob, add water, and boil it. Once we had cleaned their glass quart jars, we poured the warm corn in. We placed the lids and rings on the jars and set them into the canner which was a large metal pot with a lid that sealed when you turned it. The pressure gauge was on top of the lid. The canner held eight quart jars.

Once the jars were in the canner, we poured in water up to about ¾ of the height of the jars. We cooked it for a certain length of time, always watching the pressure gauge; then we removed the large, heavy pot from the heat. As the jars cooled the change in the temperature of the corn would suck the jar lids down a bit, thus creating a pressure sealed product. When the process ended, I had canned twenty quarts of corn for the Lacinas. The canned corn would last a year or longer. Well, I'm not really sure how long it would last. It seemed that we always ate ours up too quickly.

When Grandpa Schafer arrived for his summer visit, there was a lot of excitement. We planned a fishing trip to the lake. I packed the items we would need for cooking and eating the fish we would catch: plates, the frying pan, pot holders, the oil, and the bowl with the cornmeal and the seasonings. We also needed knives for skinning and cutting the fish. I packed other items like baby diapers, blankets for making a pallet, extra clothes, and wash cloths. We needed glasses for the water and Kool-Aid. We loved grape Kool-Aid.

Hugo gathered the poles, string, hooks, and the bait. He hitched up the mules and we loaded all this stuff into the wagon. Our mule team was really one horse and one mule. The horse was reddish in color so we called him "Old Red." The mule was a dark brown and the kids labeled him, "Old Tom." Grandpa Schafer climbed up slowly, but with a grin. The kids piled in around him. Hugo helped me and the baby, Lourene, up. Then he got in and off we went for a fun day at the lake. Even the mules seemed excited as they picked up their gait. Grandpa Schafer told stories as we rode along.

"You kids should always remember to never let your anger get the best of you. Why, I knew a guy once who got into a heated argument with a man on a construction crew. When the man spit into his lunchbox, the guy grabbed a shovel that was nearby and hit him on the head with it. And you know what?"

"What?"

"The man died, right then and there. Because he let anger get the best of him, the guy was found guilty of what they call involuntary manslaughter and he went to prison."

"But the man spit in his lunch!"

"He did. And the guy didn't mean to kill him, but he did kill him, just the same. Never let anger get control of you. I heard another story about a man who went fishing with a bunch of kids. They caught so many fish they couldn't eat them all!"

"That's us, Grandpa!"

"There was another story ....." On and on the stories went with the kids hanging on every word.

It was a very action packed occasion. Five kids ages 3, 5, 6, 8, and 10 were fishing. Butch was seventeen months old and he wanted to fish too. Watching those fish hooks, helping with baiting, taking the catch off the hooks, and reminding the kids not to get too close to the edge (we didn't want anyone to fall in) kept all three of the adults busy. But it was immensely enjoyable, just being away from the chores at home, and the work in the fields. The kids loved to go fishing and took the responsibility of the fishing pole seriously.

We didn't think of it as a biology dissection, but the kids always watched with interest as we cleaned the fish. They knew exactly what the inside of a fish looked like. The fish fry always made the trip worth the effort. The youngsters helped gather fallen tree limbs to build the fire. The fresh fish tasted so delicious when fried! This was the reward for all the effort, but who said it was effort? Catching the fish was fun!!

The World Book Encyclopedia of 1981 records that throughout the United States 780,000 women worked on farms in 1943 to raise crops needed by the Allies in Europe as World War II continued. Cotton was one of those needed crops. It was used for uniforms, coats, and blankets. We chopped and picked cotton for the neighboring growers. We were determined to make it as a family. Hugo would negotiate the price and the children and I would help him chop the cotton and then in a few weeks, pick the cotton. Sometimes we picked cotton in exchange for rent.

Over the next few years we picked cotton for Hugo's brothers Joe Hein and Leo Hein, his cousin Doc Cabron, and for others in the community. I picked in the fields nearest our home with the little ones around me and always had the baby riding on my long cotton sack, covered with a light blanket to keep the sun off or sitting, wearing a bonnet. Doc picked up the kids in his car after he picked up the black family of pickers or choppers that lived down the highway. Sometimes there were so many workers that Doc would hitch up his trailer to haul everyone. The children were helping to earn the money needed for their school supplies and for their clothes. They would sing in the fields to make the time pass as they worked.

"There's someone in the kitchen with Dinah; Someone's in the kitchen, I know, I know," "You are my sunshine, my only sunshine; You make me happy when skies are gray," "Goodnight, Irene, goodnight," and other similar songs helped them pass the time. Their Uncle Leo often sang along with them. Now and again he playfully threw the cotton bolls at the kids to interrupt their monotonous work and they would happily pepper him in return.

I taught the children how to make hats "with a purpose" out of newspaper to help keep the sun off their heads. I showed them how to double a page twice and then fold back the corners to make a triangle. When they turned up the two bottom edges, it would sit on their head neatly. I guess we were doing origami without knowing it! Making the hats "with a purpose" added fun to the morning. Besides, if they needed paper, they would have it.

Sometimes we took our lunch to the cotton patch. I would take a jar of pickles, jars of black eyed peas, and bread. I didn't even know that the vinegar and the salt in the pickles were good for you when you were sweating profusely; I just took what we had. Some land owners, like Mrs. Kotcher and Mrs. Knesek, would invite the older kids in for a delicious hot meal in the middle of the day.

We always took jars of water to the field and we got them refilled at noon. Over the years we made a lot of cotton patch memories that none of us want to talk about. Picking cotton was hot, grueling work. As the girls grew, Hugo's "little cotton pickers" (that was a term the girls didn't like to hear, but the boys teased about) were getting more beautiful.

Here were these gorgeous young girls working out in the hot sun. Dorothy was tall and slender with striking, dark brown hair. LaVerne was shorter but with long blonde hair that was nearly as white as the cotton. She had lots of natural curl, so her hair was almost bubbly. Nellene was medium in height with curly, honey blonde hair. Joyce was also medium in build, but shorter than Nellene at this point because she was younger. Joyce had blonde hair, but it was not quite as curly as Nellene's. Lourene was "cotton topped" like LaVerne, but her hair was wavy, not thick and curly. She was a tiny doll of a girl.

The little boys were growing too. Son was the blonder one of the two and both were as cute as could be. All of the kids had sparkling blue eyes. All of these beautiful kids were out in the field.

When school started in the fall the cotton picking was not yet done, so our kids had to start two weeks late. We were blessed that our youngins were bright and caught up quickly. Other children may have worked in the fields, but mine seemed to be the only ones who started school late. Sometimes the school bus would go past as they were working in the field. The girls were embarrassed as their friends waved to them, but there was nothing I could do about it. Many of the students on the bus probably thought my kids were lucky, getting to "skip school" a couple more weeks! Statistics were kept on women working on farms. I wondered how many children were helping to raise crops like cotton to aid the war effort, and then even beyond the war years.

When the crop season was over, Uncle Joe needed a few cotton related chores done. He would pay the children directly when they helped with those. It gave them a chance to have some cash of their own.

We were surviving as a family, and the kids had what they needed, barely sometimes, but enough. When the girls weren't in school they were helping with the work most of the time. The fact that they were young didn't bother me much because I had worked when I was young. It was the fact that the girls were having to do work that boys should have done that bothered me. That machete was heavy for Dorothy anyway. We had harvested the corn and we needed to salvage the stalks to feed the cows in the winter. The girls were using a machete to "wack" the tops off the corn.

Suddenly they came running toward me. They were frantic. LaVerne's finger was bleeding. Dorothy was trying to explain, "She moved her hand and I wacked it with the knife! I didn't mean to." The finger was bleeding and the fingernail had been cut through. My first aid kit was seriously lacking. The best remedy I knew of for every situation was kerosene. We hurried to the house and I dipped the finger in kerosene, wrapping it with a torn piece of an old bed sheet. My mind raced ahead to what could have happened. I hated to think of it. I had to warn them.

"Get back down there and don't be playing around," I blurted out loudly. My words seemed to hang in the air. I could sound so cold sometimes. I might have said, "Be careful," but they wouldn't have realized how serious I was. I wished I could have said, "Just come on in," but I knew the job had to be finished. I put the kerosene away and turned around. The girls were running back to the field. As I watched them go, my words were still hanging in the air.

Early the next summer, I took Joyce, Son, Butch, and Lourene on a trip to Dallas to visit Grandpa Schafer. We rode the bus and then rode on an inner urban car. The kids were intrigued by the lights all around the car. I was busy keeping up with 4 kids! Grandpa was now 73 years old. He was living with Aunt Lula and Uncle Wallace. He was still his spunky self, smoking his pipe like always.

Son fell in love with a brightly painted ceramic cat that Aunt Lula had so she gave it to him. Here I was clunking around everywhere with four kids and a large ceramic cat. Son would carry it a while, then he would set it down. He set it on the running board of the car and I was sure it would fall and break, but it survived.

When we said our good-byes, I knew we needed to get home to help with the cotton crops. I boarded the bus with an infant, 3 toddlers, and a ceramic cat.

Chapter 7

Special Times with the Grandpas

T he Christmas of 1944 was a very special one. We always tried to have fruit for Christmas and a gift for each child. Hugo would cut a cedar tree or a youpon bush with red berries from the nearby woods and decorating it was a time of family joy. This year a large package arrived early. It had been sent by Daddy. The kids were so excited. They each had a gift from their Grandpa Corley.

The suspense about those special gifts was very thick around the house. On Christmas morning there was much delight. Each of my girls had received a baby doll with eyes that would open and close. Son, now five years old, had received a small tool set. The tools were real quality, just small. There was a hammer, a saw, and a pair of pliers. He was most intrigued by the saw. Soon he was trying to saw the legs off the chairs. He was very deflated when I explained that he should saw sticks outside.

"Just sticks?" He wailed.

"Yes, sticks," I insisted. We managed to find a few old boards for him so he could try the saw and the hammer. Daddy had made this a perfect Christmas for all the children.

He came to visit the following spring. Here was my daddy, always looking sharp with his khaki pants and sport shirt. His hair was solid gray now, but it looked good on him. He was still a handsome man. All the kids enjoyed this surprise visit. Lourene, who was not quite two years old, wanted to sit on his lap all the time. Looking at those little blue eyes and those arms reaching up melted his heart every time.

The Krystenik house had two porches. While the older girls were at school Daddy would sit in a chair on the front porch just enjoying being with the younger kids, Son, Butch, and Lourene. Lourene, of course, would be sitting in his lap. One day while I was around the house washing clothes, I could hear him bantering with the kids who were making noises, trying to sound like a pig.

Son grunted. "Do I sound like a pig?" He grunted again.

"No," Daddy said.

Butch grunted with a little higher pitch. "Do I sound like a pig?"

"No."

Butch squealed. "Do I sound like a pig now?"

"Nope."

Son quickly said, "Oink! Oink! That's it! Now do I sound like a pig? Oink! Oink! Oink!"

73

"No."

Lourene joined in, "Oink, Oink!"

The kids were talking louder and faster as they tried every pig sound they knew.

Finally Daddy burst out laughing. "Only a pig can sound like a pig!" He said. He laughed and the kids giggled.

"You sure got us," Son added.

"Let me hear your pig sound again," Daddy teased.

Daddy stayed with us for several days. He visited a black man named "Gracey" who lived down the road from us. "Gracey" was the husband of Lizzie Gracy who was the midwife for me when Dorothy, LaVerne, Joyce, and Son were born. "Gracey" had worked for the railroad and needed help filling out some insurance papers and Daddy was happy to help him with the paperwork. He also talked to Hugo, suggesting that he try to get a job with the railroad.

"It is a good steady income that you can count on."

"Don't you have to travel a ways to work at times? I mean, aren't you gone from home quite a bit?" Hugo responded.

"You might be gone from home quite a bit, but the pay is good and you would be making sure that Nora Mae and the kids have what they need. Working for the railroad always allowed me to provide well for Lillian and our seven kids."

"I will think about it. Being gone from home just doesn't appeal to me."

"Maybe you could get on at the tie plant in Somerville." (Somerville, Texas was home of one of only two tie plants in the United States which made railroad ties.)

I wished Hugo would take the advice. With seven children, just doing the normal household chores is a lot, but sewing, washing, and ironing for others too....then chopping and picking cotton, well, let's just say that relief would be more than welcome.

In April of 1945 President Franklin Roosevelt died and Harry Truman became president. The war was on everyone's mind. On some days the older students were released from school to go house to house looking for metal cans. They didn't find many, but all were collected and turned in for the war effort. In May Germany surrendered. World War II was now moving to the Pacific arena.

Rationing was still in place. I had to have ration stamps to buy certain things. "If you don't need it, don't buy it" was printed on the front of the books of stamps. Even though you had a ration stamp, you still had to have money to purchase the items. The stamps just made sure that everyone had a chance to purchase the items. The short supply was caused by everything being used for the military. Rationed items were meats, butter, sugar, fats, oils, coffee, canned foods, shoes, and gasoline. We didn't have money to use all of our sugar and shoe stamps. We were instructed that any leftover stamps should be saved because they might be recalled later. (I kept some of them for more than 60 years.)

"Necessity is the mother of invention." I'm sure you have heard that. I "invented" a few things myself. I already mentioned that I used feed sacks for material to make clothes. Flour also came in cotton sacks. I saved that material too and carefully removed the seams so the material would remain intact. I had an idea and I tried it. I bleached out the printing on the white flour sacks and sewed five of them together and it worked! It fit our bed mattresses. There you go – we had bed sheets made from flour sacks! When cut just right those flour sacks could be sewed into white Sunday shirts for Hugo and the boys. Let's see, those wonderful flour sacks also became the boys underwear or cup towels for the kitchen.

I figured out how to curl the girls' hair. We didn't own any hair rollers, but with five girls you have to have curls, so this is what I did. While the hair was still wet from being washed I wound it around a pencil up close to the head like you would wind it around a hair roller. Then I put a five inch piece of string or a five inch by one inch strip of material through the looped hair and tied it. I pulled the pencil out leaving the string tied in until the hair was completely dry. Every string worked like a hair roller. When the hair was dry and I removed the string, the hair hung in ringlets.

We moved again and our Saturday "Sunday" School ended. Two missionaries who talked about faraway places had recently visited. They brought a snake skin that was four inches wide and really long. I don't think my kids will ever forget those two ladies. This time we moved to Pivonka's Hill. The kids would now attend High Prairie School. They walked through the woods carrying their lunches. After eighth grade Dorothy was bussed to Somerville High School. High Prairie School was eventually phased out and all the kids went to Somerville schools.

The Pivonka house had two large bedrooms downstairs and a small attic bedroom upstairs. There was a kitchen on the back, with a small shed attached to the side of the kitchen. A large porch went all across the front of the house. There was also a barn with a cow pen. To pay our rent Hugo agreed to cut trees down, make logs, and then quarter the logs. The owner of the property planned to sell the wood as fence posts. The house had no electricity, but we had never had it so that was no big deal. I was still using a wood stove for cooking. In the winter my kitchen was always warm and cozy, but in the summer it was a hot and stifling place.

I knew that Grandpa Schafer would soon be arriving on the bus for his summer visit. He had sent a letter saying that he wanted to visit Mama when he came and I knew that we would have to drive the wagon over. Our wagon was open; we didn't have the luxury of a covering like the Conestoga wagons had.

Because the sun could be so hot, I determined that I would make new bonnets for the girls to keep the sun off their heads. That's what I did. When Grandpa arrived one of the first things we did was go to the Brinkmann place.

We parked the wagon at the road and walked in so our animals would not mess up the long dirt lane. All the girls were wearing their new matching, red gingham bonnets. They looked dressed for a party!

Mama was happy to see us all. Most of her brood was gone from home now. She had only the youngest three at home, Lena, now 19, Hubert, now 17, and Nellie Faye, now 15. Mama's eyes were starting to get bad. Her glasses were thicker than the last time I'd seen her. We laughed and talked and enjoyed the day. Grandpa talked of days gone by and fun times we'd had. We headed home before dark so "Old Red" and "Old Tom" could see the way.

The next morning we loaded all the necessary gear into the wagon and went to Courtney Lake to fish. There were always adventures when Grandpa was here. We got the trot line set and were spreading our blanket to sit down when someone noticed the cork go under the water. Hugo and the kids ran to see what we had caught. There was a large turtle as well as two small fish on the line. Hugo took the fish off, but he couldn't get the hook out of the turtle's mouth. Grandpa tried, but he couldn't get it out either.

"Guess I'll have to cut his head off to even get it off the line," Hugo said.

"Looks like it."

Hugo got the hatchet and chopped off the turtle's head. The bleeding turtle started running without its head. Everyone jumped back. The turtle ran across Butch's foot and left a lot of blood on his little foot. Butch started screaming hysterically. He thought that the turtle had bit his foot off. Super girl to the rescue! (Super Girl didn't really come on the scene until 1959; guess I was early.)

I ran and grabbed Butch up. I splashed his feet in the lake and then carried him back to the blanket. Once he could see his foot, still attached, with no blood on it, he was okay. He even smiled. The turtle's muscle spasms had played out. He lay dead. All was well. We cleaned the soft shell turtle and cut him up, later frying him along with the good number of fish we took. We relished the cook-out, and arrived home tired and ready for sleep.

Grandpa Schafer left for Dallas and it was time for us to chop cotton. This summer we would work for Bill Gaas and Frank Schmiller as well as Doc, Leo, and Joe. Doc's cotton was planted in the bottom land nearer Courtney Lake. It rained and we held our breath. We knew that too much rain would flood and ruin the cotton. We needed this income. Frank Schmiller's cotton was in the Brazos River bottom. We were so happy that it didn't flood. I always worked in the cotton fields that were closest to home, with the small children near me. The older kids would work for Gaas and Schmiller.

We chopped cotton from "sun up" to almost "sun down." Each day when we got home I started immediately on supper. Some nights I had clothes to wash that we needed to wear the next day. Regularly we had to get bread made for the next day. Once one of the girls prepared the dough, I had to wait for it to rise before I could bake it. The coals in the stove needed to be just right so it would bake evenly. My pan held three loaves of bread. The girls had learned to make really smooth bread.

If the kids were still awake when it came out of the oven (usually they were not), they would beg for warm pieces with butter. I couldn't let them eat tomorrow's bread, but a warm buttered half slice brought a thousand smiles. Sometimes when the dough was first ready, I would break off pieces, fry it, and then sprinkle sugar on it to make a yummy sweet treat. During the cotton season my sleep seemed extremely short.

On August 6 and August 9 of 1945 atomic bombs were dropped on Hiroshima and Nagasaki. Japan surrendered on September 1 and World War II was over. We read the newspaper as much as we could to learn all about it. At this point we had no radio, television, or telephone. We occasionally bought newspapers; usually we got them from others who had finished with them. Aunt Minnie Schumacher got the paper first, then Grandma Hein read it, then we got it.

Hugo loved to read the paper. I did too, but usually did not have much time for reading because the children and the household chores kept me busy; but the war was over! We were so happy about that! We devoured the newspapers. Our nation was strong. We felt proud and we empathized with those who had lost family members in the war. Some people were celebrating; their loved ones were coming home. We had cousins and uncles coming home. The United

States military demobilized and the armed forces quickly went from 12 million to 2 million. When the kids started school that fall all the book covers had the picture of General Douglas MacArthur, who had led the successful Pacific offensive, on the front.

In 1946 Grandpa Schafer visited in the spring. He was sitting in a chair on the front porch and Son, Butch, and Lourene were around the corner on the ground. They were playing a sort of "peek-a-boo" game with him.

"Grandpa, we see you!" They called out and then ducked behind the corner so he couldn't see them.

Grandpa looked around. "Who's calling me?"

There was silence. In a couple of minutes they popped out and called again, "Grandpa we see you!" They ducked behind the corner.

He leaned his chair back a bit to try to catch them, but he still couldn't see them. "Who's calling me? I know I heard someone."

The kids were as quiet as a mouse. They waited. The third time they called he leaned farther back in the chair. Suddenly Grandpa Schafer and the chair fell off of the porch!

The kids were scared. They came running around to the kitchen where I was cooking.

"Mama! Mama! Grandpa Schafer fell off the porch! He's lying on the ground!"

"What?" My heart skipped a beat. "Where is he?" Grandpa was now 75 years old. Too old to be falling, I knew.

I ran and followed them around to the front. Grandpa was lying flat on the ground with the chair lying beside him. I was pretty shook up.

"Are you okay? What happened?"

He started to roll over. He kept rubbing himself all over – his legs, his arms, his head. He spoke deliberately.

"I guess I'm okay."

He got up very slowly, checking himself again. He winked at the kids, "I thought I heard someone around the corner." Then he smiled. We all relaxed. We knew Grandpa was okay.

Before he left, Grandpa talked to Hugo about getting a job with the railroad.

"You should inquire about it. It is a good steady income," he said.

"I will think on it."

Thursday, September 12, 1946 seemed like an ordinary day. I was washing clothes when Mr. Pivonka came to the front door. I hurried around the house to see what he needed. He paused and shook his head.

Chapter 8

My World Keeps Changing

The date was September 12, 1946. Mr. Pivonka spoke slowly, "Nora Mae, I'm sorry to bring you bad news." Hugo was coming across the yard so he waited for him to join us. "Your sister from Dallas called and said to tell you that your Daddy's dead," he paused. "There was a terrible accident. He was run over by a freight train. She left a phone number for you."

My mind started racing. It didn't make sense; it was so unlikely that Daddy would be run over by the train. Why, he had worked for the railroad for twenty-eight years. He knew all the safety stuff. He had trained many others – surely they were mistaken. It must be someone else.

"Did she say how it happened?"

"No. She only said that it happened this morning at the railroad yards in Corsicana. Again, I'm so sorry."

It seemed like time stood still. I felt numb. "Thanks for bringing the message," I mumbled.

"Take care," he said as he slowly walked away.

Hugo said to me, "If we hurry we can be ready before the bus passes by. We can catch a ride to Caldwell to use a phone to call your sister."

There was no one to watch Butch and Lourene so we took them along and went to call my sister Sarah Castloo who told us that the railroad workers had been staying at the Southern Pacific switch yards in Corsicana. Daddy had found his foreman dead in the bed this morning and was on his way to report the death. Evidently his mind was so preoccupied that he did not hear the train as he crossed the tracks and he was killed instantly. Daddy was the assistant foreman on the bridge gang. The burial would be on Saturday afternoon in Gilmer, Texas.

Life can be so harsh. Or I could say that life can bring us blessings. I had known Daddy for sixteen of my thirty years. During that time, I always felt the support of his love. I am eternally grateful for what he planted into my family; as suddenly as he appeared, he was gone; but his influence was monumental.

Hugo and I took the bus to Gilmer to be with my family. It was a closed casket because Daddy had been cut in pieces by the train wheels; he was in a plastic bag. I was going to miss him, but I vowed that I would stay in touch with my sisters Sarah Castloo and Dorothy Jones in order to keep up with everyone. Daddy had made me feel that he wanted my family to be a part of his family.

It seemed like I was deep in thought quite a bit after I returned home from the funeral. Death affects us in different ways. It was hard for a person like me to cry openly; there was always someone that needed me to be strong. I found myself always trying to be the constant in the storm, because I felt that I had to be.

I was cleaning up leaves by the garden fence. Surely here I could relax just a little. My mind wandered...

"Ouch!!" What was that? I looked down and saw two tiny dots on my right hand between my middle and pointer fingers.

A snake bite! I saw the culprit as he slithered under the brace at the corner fence post. It was a copperhead snake. I knew this was a serious situation. Hugo was not at home. I grabbed my wrist, holding the hand down and squeezing tightly. I bolted to the house; the kids were behind me.

"What is it, Mama?"

"What's wrong?"

I put my hand in the kerosene oil. The girls saw the two holes where the snake fangs had penetrated the skin.

"Run, quickly! I need Mrs. Gaas to take me to the doctor! It was a copperhead snake." The children felt the urgency in my tone. The little ones began to cry.

Dorothy immediately took control of the situation, "LaVerne and Nell, go get Mrs. Gaas. I will watch the kids. Run!" She cuddled Butch and Lourene.

LaVerne and Nellene sprinted the whole way, across the highway and up the hill. When Dorothy Gaas opened the door, Nell was so out of breath and so traumatized that she could not speak.

Dorothy Gaas pointed. "Matilda's out in the field." Matilda who could drive saw LaVerne dashing across the field and came to meet her.

"Mama's been bitten by a copperhead!"

"Let's go!" Matilda loaded the girls in the car and came to get me. I was sitting on the porch, still holding my wrist down, with my hand in the kerosene.

"Don't worry, Mama. We're okay," Dorothy called as I jumped into the car. Matilda drove as fast as she dared to Dr. Pazdral in Somerville. I felt dizzy, but managed to stay focused.

Dr. Pazdral laughed about me using the kerosene oil. He immediately gave me a shot. He cut an X on the area and attempted to suck out the poison with a syringe. He told me that it was a miracle that I did not get deathly sick and vomit.

We went home. My swollen arm was so heavy that I could not lift it, therefore, I was wearing a sling. Mr. Gaas had found and killed the copperhead. When Hugo got home he went back out to that fence post and shoveled through the leaves. He said, "Snakes come in pairs, you know." Sure enough, he found a second copperhead and killed it too. I got over the ordeal with no complications.

During the years that we lived on Pivonka's Hill my four oldest girls all completed confirmation classes. Some of my proudest moments as a parent were when they were confirmed.

Dorothy attended confirmation classes first. She would ride the Texas Bus Lines bus to Aunt Minnie Schoppe's (Hugo's sister) in Somerville and spend the night. She would attend Reverend Modschiedler's confirmation class on Wednesday, spend another night, and then take the bus home on Thursday. When she completed all of the training I took her to Caldwell to a beauty shop to get her first permanent. I also bought her a new white dress and on confirmation day she looked splendid as the whole family attended her big occasion!

Later Reverend Hans Nottrot drove a station wagon (which the church purchased) to pick up all the kids for confirmation classes. Rev. Nottrot pastored four country churches so he had a rotating schedule for the services. Service times at each church rotated also. One Sunday service would begin at 10:00 AM; the next Sunday, the service would start at 2:00 PM; the next Sunday it started at 6:00 PM. On the fourth Sunday of the rotation, the congregation stayed home and the head of every household was expected to teach the Bible lesson to the family. Each of the churches rotated through the schedule so everyone got to have a Sunday morning service at least once a month.

Two years after Dorothy was confirmed Rev. Nottrot drove the station wagon to pick up LaVerne and Nellene for confirmation classes which met each week on Wednesday evening. I ordered them identical dresses from a catalog. When the package arrived it was not the dresses we had ordered; but they did fit and there was not time to return and reorder; so we kept them. Their dresses were deep blue with red trim at the bottom, a little dark for wearing under the white confirmation robes, but special new dresses, nonetheless. Joyce's confirmation dress was turquoise (the right order came). She was confirmed in 1951.

My girls were beautiful, smart, and spunky. They seemed to have developed my instinct for survival. Dorothy loved to read, particularly mysteries, and to do book reports. LaVerne was blessed with the same knack for numbers that possessed me. Nellene was adventurous, analytical, and straight to the point. She was taller than LaVerne and she was strong. She often helped Hugo pull the two handled saw when he was cutting down the trees to help pay our rent. Joyce had her father's witty personality. The girls supported each other and stuck together.

At confirmation, I was always glad for the girls. I had kept my promise to teach them about God, and therefore felt a sense of accomplishment; but something was wrong – I felt like I was still not right with God, but I didn't know what to do about it.

When Hugo bought a black 1925 Model T car we were excited! We were finally joining the ranks of the mobile society, nevermind that the vehicle was almost twenty years old. Henry Ford's dream of a car for the masses had finally trickled down to us. This Model T had a trunk on the back with a lid like a tool box. When we loaded up to go anywhere Hugo and I and the baby were seated in the front and the rest of the kids were sardined in the back seat. This old car was a mechanic's nightmare! It broke down constantly, but Hugo knew how to work on it.

The first time he took the thing all apart he could not remember how to put it back together. We panicked. We had to get help to put it back together. After that, whenever Hugo worked on the car, I stood and watched. I guess we made a good pair; he knew how and what to repair, and once I had seen the parts removed from their place, I could tell him exactly how to put them back together.

Now that Hugo had a car he was able to get a job as a security guard for the railroad tie plant at Somerville. It seemed like he was always wrestling with that car. The tires were the worst! During the war all the rubber was sent to the war effort. Because there were no new inner tubes to be found, we had to patch and re-patch the old ones. If Hugo had a flat, the kids would take the tube to Sablatura's Store to get it patched. Finally the guys at the store told the kids that there was no way to patch the tube anymore. They couldn't fix this blow-out; the tube was shot! Hugo was not to be grounded. He stuffed straw into the tire, wired it up, and drove it like that! Synthetic rubber was such a blessing when it was invented.

I really wanted to drive. I figured that if millions of people could do it, I could do it. The Model T had to be primed to achieve a richer fuel mixture before you started it. It was built in such a way that you could start it using the battery and hand crank or you could use the electric starter which was under the floor. The starter button triggered 6 volts from the magnetos (which were large v-shaped magnets arranged in a circle). The distributor would convert the 6 volts from the magnetos to 20,000 volts which would fire the spark plugs. There were two separate "on" position choices for the key because of the two different ways to start the engine. After you got it running, it was best to turn the key to "magneto" so you could save on the battery.

The car had three foot pedals together on the floor. The right pedal was the brake; the middle one was reverse; the left pedal was similar to a clutch and operated the two gears – low and high. All three pedals and the electric starter were operated by the feet. Once you started the car you set the timing of the engine by using a spark advance on the left side of the steering wheel. The throttle was on the right side of the steering wheel. There also was a hand brake lever on the floor on the driver's left. It worked in conjunction with the left foot pedal to control the low gear and high gear. All of this was a lot to think about, but I was sure I could do it!

I convinced Hugo to let me drive to Caldwell one day. The start was smooth. We hadn't gone very far when there was a loud banging noise.

Hugo yelled, "Nora Mae!" and I had to pull off the road and into the ditch. After investigating Hugo determined that a loose screw had somehow gotten in the magnetos. I had nothing to do with a loose screw getting in the magnetos, but the Model T had to be worked on, so my driving window of opportunity was closed. It was too risky to let me drive – why anything could happen! I still wanted to drive. I still had hope. It was a dream that I kept alive for a very long time.

The Pivonka place was in the country. It intrigued me that the water from the well there was always cold. Because we had no electricity we could not refrigerate meat. We joined a Co-op Beef Club group in which families went together to butcher an animal and share the meat so that all of it would be consumed fairly quickly. We had chickens so we had eggs regularly. With no way to refrigerate meat a chicken had to be butchered shortly before you wanted to cook it. I had to chop the chicken's head off; there was a tree stump near the wood pile that I used for this task. I know, it's yucky, but my kids needed good protein to eat. Surgeons put up with yuck for the good of the patient; I did it as a good dietician.

Once the chicken was butchered we had to pluck the feathers. We saved the soft feathers to use in making pillows or featherbed quilts. After cleaning the feathers off I singed the bird's skin to get off the tiniest feather fuzz. Then

I could cut the chicken up for frying or I could boil it whole until tender for making chicken and dumplings. Delicious!

In the summer we had to have the windows of the house open despite the fact that there were no window screens. We didn't have problems with mosquitoes and other insects coming in, but one morning LaVerne had a memorable awakening. During the night, a cat had brought kittens and deposited them on her pillow. LaVerne awoke to find kittens on her head. Such adventure we could have done without!

All the kids slept in one of the downstairs bedrooms until we finally moved Dorothy and LaVerne upstairs. On bright nights Dorothy would sit in the upstairs window and read her book by moonlight.

When Grandpa Schafer came to visit in the summer of 1947, we all piled into the Model T for a fishing trip to the lake on Aunt Minnie Schumacher's place. We put all the supplies into the trunk and all the kids migrated to the car. Son was sitting on the floor in front of Grandpa. It was a very bumpy ride across the pasture and Grandpa's pipe (he always had that pipe) kept hitting Son on the top of his head and he was giving out a little "oh" or "ouch" on every bounce. He started trying to duck, but the pipe inevitably hit him anyway. There were so many legs and feet on the floor that he was pretty much hemmed in. After each little "oh" I could hear Grandpa's needling, "I'm not doing that; your Daddy's doing that!"

In the evenings Grandpa loved to play dominoes with my four oldest girls. They kept winning the games. He finally figured out that they were actually cheating. They knew this old set of dominoes by the scratches on the back of each one. When he realized he was being duped, he angrily shoved all his dominoes to the middle of the table and said roughly, "I'm going to bed!" The next morning though, he was all smiles again. These great grandkids of his were a pretty sharp bunch.

On April 9 of 1948 my third son was born. I named him Tillman after the doctor who delivered him. Tillman Lloyd Hein was kid number eight for me and there was a lot of excitement in the house celebrating this little guy.

Less than a month later, on May 8, Grandpa Schafer died at the age of seventy-seven. He had been my life line, my anchor; sometimes I felt like the twinkle in his eye. I was thirty-two years old and had been his first grandchild. Hugo and I took Tillman and went to Dallas for the funeral. I was saying good-bye to all the love and laughter he had shared with my family. I was saying good-bye to a dear friend. I grieved deeply, but my tiny new baby kept my focus on the future. I could so profoundly see that life is made of changes. The changes we embrace determine the demeanor that radiates from us.

I was in for more big changes.

Chapter 9

Awakening!

Shortly after Tillman was born the kids started telling me that Butch was sleepwalking. They said that he was going out the window at night and then coming back in later. I asked him about it.

"I've never done that," he declared.

I thought that perhaps the kids were making it up. One night I heard a kicking noise at the front door. Hugo and I wondered who was coming in the middle of the night. When someone kicked again we cautiously opened the door to find Butch who was seven years old standing there with an egg in each hand. He had already been to the chicken pen! I took the eggs and put him back to bed. The next morning he didn't remember that he had gone out the window nor that he had brought the eggs.

The kids laughed. "We told you, Mama. He always goes out through the window and he comes back in through the bedroom door. It's like a routine."

Butch had this reply, "I don't believe you; I would know if I had done that."

I began to try to listen for him; there was no particular pattern, but randomly he would sleepwalk. The kids always told me after it happened, but I never heard him go out.

Four of the kids shared that bedroom. Joyce and Nell slept in one bed and Son and Butch slept in the bed by the window, but Son wouldn't realize Butch was gone until he would hear him getting back in bed. One night when it had rained Butch got back in bed with muddy feet. In the early morning light Son could see the mud on their white sheets. He made Butch get up and wipe his feet off. Later when Butch awakened he couldn't deny that he had been outside because the evidence was on the sheets. He didn't remember it, but now he knew that he did sleepwalk.

Butch also talked in his sleep. The kids would tease him about it continuously. One night he kept saying, "There's a big noodle under the soup!" He kept repeating it and he sounded frightened. His talking woke the kids and they asked him questions about it.

"What does it look like?"

"Just how big is it?"

"What kind of soup is it?"

He just kept repeating, "There's a big noodle under the soup!" And he was getting louder and more agitated. The kids were laughing and snickering. Finally they settled down and went back to sleep. Henry never remembered anything about it, not even a dream about a big noodle.

In April of 1949 LaVerne became seriously ill. She had to be hospitalized in Galveston which was 150 miles away. With seven other kids at home and one of those a baby, I could not go. Reverend Nottrot drove Hugo to admit her in the hospital. Dorothy went along for moral support. LaVerne had a major infection in the lining of her abdomen, very near her appendix. She spent three full weeks in the hospital with a tube through the abdomen to drain the infection.

It took a trip to Caldwell to even call and check on her. My heart so wanted to go, but I could not. I continuously prayed for her, sent her cards, and mailed her a box of Easter egg candy. Finally she came home with this caution from the doctor, "Her appendix is probably affected because of the proximity of that infection. She will more than likely need an operation later."

In May Dorothy graduated from Somerville High School. She was only sixteen years old. She had skipped third grade the year they added grade 12. She was a great student; she listened; and she loved to read. Because she listened she made high grades on all the tests; so high in fact they had her skip 5th grade at High Prairie School. She had skipped two grades and still maintained excellent marks.

Daddy had sent the kids a set of books for Christmas one year. Dorothy read them all. We didn't have many books at our house; the older kids all read those books and Dorothy and I read them to the younger ones. When she took the eighth grade achievement test she was the only student who passed the Reading section. Her friends all thought she had cheated. She explained to me that all the pieces of literature they were tested on were stories from the book set her Grandpa Corley had given us. One of the pieces tested was "The Owl and the Pussycat Went to Sea." Dorothy had that one memorized. She practically knew all those books by heart.

Dorothy was a real leader. She was also a visionary. Some of her friends had gone to the city (Houston) when they graduated high school. She had heard about their jobs. They were actually making money! She wanted to get a real job and never pick cotton again. She was tired of the cotton burrs cutting her fingers. Her teachers had done a good job of helping her realize she was qualified for the opportunity that was out there. After graduation she borrowed $7.50 from her Grandma Hein and took the bus to Houston. She and her high school friends Annie Mae and Evelyn Ondrasek got a place together. My little girl was on her way.

The small hole in LaVerne's abdomen healed quickly and she joined the rest of us picking cotton. Hugo was working at the tie plant so without him and Dorothy it was taking us longer to do the work; however, less cotton was now being planted. Thirty days from the day LaVerne came home from the hospital she became deathly sick and had to be hospitalized again. Her appendix had burst; she had an emergency appendectomy in Galveston. Her hospital stay was 19 days this time and our hearts rejoiced when she returned home well.

Hugo's brother Raymond and his wife Melinda had twins that same year, a boy named Dayle and a girl named Gayle. It was happy news. Ever since I knew my Daddy and Lillian had had a set of twins, I had wished that I would have a set of twins, secretly of course. I never told anyone; they would have thought that I was nuts.

When Dorothy went to the city, it was like she was in another world. The homes in the city, including the duplex where she lived, had electricity and indoor plumbing. She got a job which meant she could buy new clothes. Her heart strings were still tied to us. As a family we had always worked for each other. She wanted her family to be able to enjoy a few modern things too. She visited home as soon as she could. It wasn't long until she came home and found electric wires on the floor of the upstairs bedroom; it was the wiring for the lights downstairs. Electricity had finally reached our rural area; it was 1949.

That Christmas Dorothy gave us a radio and an iron. She connected us to the world and we all looked much spiffier with our pressed clothes. What an improvement it was over the iron we heated on the wood stove. At first we had no wall plugs; the cords were plugged into the small light bulb fixtures.

The girls were intrigued by Dorothy's stories about the city. Her first job was at Walgreen's Drug Store; then she got a job at Southwestern Bell Telephone Company. It didn't take them long to discover that she was a gifted leader. The girls couldn't wait to go to the city themselves; my little birds seemed to be trying to get out of the nest. When the spring semester ended in 1950, LaVerne and Nell went to Houston to get summer jobs. Dorothy had invited them to stay with her for the summer. They both got jobs at Weingarten's which was a large grocery store. Besides groceries Weingarten's also had a drug department, a tobacco department, a bakery, a clothing section, and a lunch counter. The gossip started almost immediately; I am not positive who started it.

"Did you hear about Hugo and Nora Mae's girls?"

"No. What?"

"They're selling wine. They went to Houston and they're working in a place called Wine Gardens!"

"Really?"

"Yes! LaVerne and Nellene went for the summer."

"Are you sure? Selling wine?"

"Yes. Yes. I overheard Hugo talking to them on the phone. He came and borrowed my phone the other day."

"Why, you don't say. I told them those girls would get out of hand if they weren't more strict with them. Poor Nora Mae!"

On and on it went, like gossip does. They had confused Weingarten's with Wine Gardens. By the time the girls came home to visit they were being labeled "those wild Hein girls!" LaVerne was given a job at the tobacco counter; Nell was assigned to the bakery which infuriated her. She did not want to work with "the old ladies" so she found herself a more exciting job at the Greyhound Coffee Shop.

I gave birth to my ninth child in July. Hugo's mom named the splendid little girl Virginia Ann. I was exasperated, to say the least, when Hugo quit his job at the Somerville tie plant. By the end of July we were struggling to pay our bills; now we also had an electric bill to pay. The girls were sending money to help us.

At the end of the summer LaVerne came home to go to school for the fall semester. Dorothy had graduated high school and that was LaVerne's dream too. She was devastated to find that we had almost nothing to eat and Hugo was unemployed. After a few days she went and called Dorothy who told her that Southwestern Bell was hiring some part-time positions and one full-time position. LaVerne met the qualifications so she returned to Houston; she got the full-time job.

About the same time Nell decided that she wanted to stay in the city. Shortly after LaVerne returned to Houston, Nell caught the bus home and asked Hugo if she could stay in Houston. "It's a lot easier than picking cotton, Dad. The coffee shop even has air conditioning," she reasoned, "I am making good money."

"If that's what you want to do and you're making enough money to take care of yourself, you can do it," he told her.

I was so torn inside. Nell was so young! She was fourteen years old. I couldn't argue with the fact that she was making more money than she would if she came home. And, I had been fourteen when I left home. Still...to be so far away...I worried about her...so young...and she was so pretty.

The dynamics in the house changed enormously. We were down to six children at home. When I had given birth to Virginia, the birth was not as smooth as usual for me. Dr. Tillman Dodd advised us that I should not have any more children. We were wearing out my "baby factory." He said, "Nora Mae, if you have another baby, there is a very big chance you will die."

Early the next year Hugo got a job with the railroad; he was sent to work in Oklahoma. With him gone so much it was difficult for me and the kids to get to church at all. I began listening to the radio on Sundays. One Sunday afternoon I heard a woman from Hempstead, Texas named Frances Stork preaching. She had a simple way of explaining things. I liked it and began to listen to her program every week.

We moved to Frank Mynar's place. I had to withdraw and enroll the kids in school again; this time they would attend Second Creek School. Frank Mynar was the uncle of Butch's friend Bennie Mynar. Butch was excited to live near Bennie.

Son and Butch played with him and Lourene usually went along. It seemed like the boys (my boys and their friends) were always picking on Lourene. She was just 16 months behind Butch, but she was still the little sister. She was eight years old.

The kids went to Alma and Ed Mynar's house for Bennie's birthday party. On the way home Son and Butch were teasing Lourene and laughing at her. She was getting angry and they would not let up. She had a cup of ice in her hand so she threw a piece of ice at Butch. He tried to duck but it caught him in the eyebrow; of course, it bled a lot. He had a scar there for the rest of his life. The teasing ended … for the moment.

One night someone tried to get in the back door of the house. The kids and I had gone to bed; Hugo was in Oklahoma. The noise was loud enough that everyone woke up, scared. I grabbed the broom and went to the door they were messing with. I stamped the broom on the floor and with as much authority as I could muster, I shouted in a low tone, "We will not open the door. Get out of here now." They immediately ran.

It must have been some hobos who were routinely stopping off here to sleep. They were expecting an empty house; I had scared them as much as they had scared us. They bolted across the yard without looking back. Even Virginia awakened and was now crying. It took a while to settle everyone down, but after I told them that I thought it had been hobos, they were comforted.

There was a huge shift in our way of life when Dorothy bought us a refrigerator! Our milk would stay fresh longer; meat could be frozen and thawed to cook. The kids enjoyed the luxury of having ice readily available (ice made in trays, there were no icemakers yet); we could even buy ice cream to bring home and eat later. Buying a chicken that was packaged and ready to cook was such an extravagance when compared to my having to butcher, pluck feathers, and singe one!

In 1951 people stood in line in New York City to buy hand mixers. Before World War II home appliances were unaffordable for the common consumer; after the war they were unavailable. More families were now getting to enjoy many of the blessings made possible by electricity.[3]

One Sunday afternoon I was listening to my electric radio. I was feeling pretty down this day, but listened intently because it seemed like she was talking to me. All of a sudden I saw it! I don't know why I never saw it before. I had read it many times, but when Sister Stork read John 3:16 and 17 from the Bible something clicked inside me: "whosoever" meant me! Maybe I had too many responsibilities before, maybe I was too tired to ever hear it, maybe a baby was always needing attention; whatever had kept me blinded, it was now gone. I could really see that "whosoever" meant me.

"For God so loved the world that he gave his only begotten Son, that whosoever believeth in him should not perish, but have everlasting life.

"For God sent not his Son into the world to condemn the world; but that the world through him might be saved." (KJV)

I heard her saying something else, "If thou shalt confess with thy mouth the Lord Jesus, and shalt believe in thine heart that God hath raised Him from the dead, thou shalt be saved." This was Romans 10:9 (KJV).

Confess your belief! She said, "Confess to Jesus and confess to others." That was what I had been missing. As the radio program ended and I prayed with her, a peace engulfed me. I will never forget Sister Stork. I couldn't wait to get to church to confess to others.

I accompanied my kids to the church nearest us. It was where Hugo's sister Emma and her husband Wayne Norville attended. Joyce and Lourene had gone first, walking the entire way. This day, we all went and at the end of the service everyone stood. When the preacher invited people to come forward if they wanted to accept Jesus, I walked to the front of the church; several people were standing there. I timidly told the pastor, "I want to confess that I believe in Jesus as my Savior. I do believe that God raised him from the dead." I spoke slowly.

When he took my hand tears began to flow from my eyes. They wouldn't stop. It was like the catharsis that Shakespeare tried to accomplish with his tragedies; only this was deeper. It wasn't someone else's tragedy that I was crying for, it was my own sins – all the mistakes I had made, all the hardships I'd experienced, the anger I had felt, the hurt I'd suppressed, the doubt. I confessed it all. I couldn't stop this river of tears; but it was somehow miraculously washing me. I felt so clean! It seemed that Jesus had wrapped His arms around me. I was so small, so INSIGNIFICANT, but the great God of the universe loved me.

But, oh! I was crying in church. I hadn't meant to. I covered my face with my hands; someone handed me some tissues. When my weeping finally stopped, I was amazed! The people in this church didn't seem to care. Some of my kids were embarrassed, but no one else seemed to care. A fountain of joy that I'd never experienced before was rolling from deep down inside of me. My circumstances had not changed, but for the first time I felt that all was right between me and my creator. It seemed that my soul had just awakened from a 37-year slumber. I wanted to sing!

But what about Hugo; he'd always been so jealous of me. More than once when he was gone overnight he, upon returning, had checked for footprints outside our bedroom window to see if someone had sneaked in to visit me. Now that he was working in Oklahoma, would he approve of me going to church every week? I didn't think so, but I had a lot of hope. I couldn't help smiling.

The deep joy that I felt that day didn't go away. I looked like the same person, but I was so changed on the inside. I began to pray that we would move closer to a church, close enough that we could walk there – regularly.

Chapter 10

Eleven? You're kidding, right?

W ith Hugo working out of town the kids and I inherited all of the family chores; one, of which, was
burning the trash. I had lit the fire, but couldn't tell you why
the flames spread. There was no time to think about that; I
had to figure out how to get the fire out. It seemed like the
wind picked up and before I knew it the patch of woods was
on fire. I sent one of the kids to get the Mynars while the
rest of us started fighting the fire with water buckets and wet
blankets. With the Mynars help we got the fire put out, but
a large wooded area was charred.

When Hugo came home, Frank Mynar told him that he
was needing the house back; we would have to move. Hugo
couldn't believe it. We had resided here less than a year.
We had lived on Pivonka's Hill for eight years and when we
moved here we had thought that we would be staying for a
while. Hugo was downright angry about it. He decided that

since we had to move he would move us to town. With him working out of town it would be more convenient for the family to get groceries, etc.

Joyce who was the oldest child at home, would be starting high school in the fall. Hugo asked her if she would rather go to Somerville High School or Caldwell High School and she answered, "Somerville High School." Hugo looked for and found an available house in Somerville. We couldn't be choosey; we needed a place. We moved to the old Webush house on the corner of 10th Street and Avenue D. The house was in poor shape, but it was within walking distance of several churches. My prayer had been answered! God was working as He had been all along, only I couldn't see it before.

Sister Stork's sister, Alice Williams, pastored a church that was only two blocks from us. We chose to go there. Sister Stork and Sister Williams were preachers before women preachers were socially acceptable. They were used to having to prove themselves in a male dominated field. Sister Williams had a strong will to preach and she was not afraid to pray for anything – if you had a need and asked her to pray, she would do it. Over the years she prayed for many people in our small town. She didn't care if you attended her church or not; if you asked for prayer, she prayed.

Other pastors sent people to her if needs were extreme. She was occasionally awakened in the night when someone was desperate to reach heaven. She felt that desperate people were serious about prayer. Race did not matter to her; she prayed for all. More than once people outside the church came asking for deliverance for a demon possessed victim. When she prayed Jesus supernaturally released them. She had earned the respect of the other preachers in town and was a part of the community ministerial alliance. It was not uncommon for her to teach at ministerial gatherings just as often as the other ministers.

When we first came to Somerville we didn't know all of that; we just knew that her church was two blocks from our house. She and her husband Lanie Williams had two sons near the age of Joyce. That was a plus and she believed in providing activities for the church youth. When I discovered that Sister Williams was Sister Stork's sister, I definitely felt at home at the Apostolic Faith Church.

Hugo complained about me and the kids going to church on Sunday. He said that lunch was never ready on time. I started cutting up a chicken early on Sunday and baking it on a very low temperature. It would be ready when we got home. I also peeled the potatoes early in the morning and let them set in water. They cooked after church while the kids helped me set the table and get the drinks.

Soon Hugo was going with us to church on the Sundays that he didn't work. The Apostolic Faith Church had morning and evening services on Sunday. Most of the men in the congregation worked at the Somerville tie plant so some men were off on Tuesday and some were off on Friday. They did not want to miss mid-week service so to accommodate them

Sister Williams had a service on Tuesday night and one on Friday night. We started going to both of those services. It wasn't long and I was singing with the choir and teaching Sunday School. Hugo made his own profession of faith in Jesus Christ.

When Dwight Eisenhower was elected as President of the United States in November of 1952, my half-brother Ruel Hughes Corley, Jr was assigned duty as navigator for the president's plane, Air Force One. I remained navigator of the Hugo Hein plane and its expanding crew. When I realized that I was pregnant again I became terribly afraid because I knew what the doctor had told me. I could hear it as if it were yesterday,

"Nora Mae, if you have another baby, there is a very big chance you will die."

I asked Sister Williams to pray for me and the baby, which she did and the fear which had engulfed me, lifted. I was in church regularly and when I went into labor, I was not afraid. Hugo got Bessie Hawthorne to give me a ride to the hospital, but rats!! I hadn't washed Hugo's underwear yet and he needed to head back to Oklahoma this evening. I asked Bessie to stop at JC Penny's in Brenham so I could buy some underwear for him. She did and then took me to Sarah B. Milroy Hospital and my tenth child, who was born about twenty minutes after I arrived there, became my first child to be born in a hospital. Bessie exclaimed, "Nora Mae, if I had known the delivery was that close, I would never have stopped at Penny's!"

There was no rejoicing from family and friends when the last of our children were born. Joyce felt degraded when citizens approached her at the café about taking up a collection for a hysterectomy for "her mother." On this day our friends at church did not say much, except Perry Hawthorne who made Hugo angry when he commented, "It's just another ugly, red-faced girl." In contrast, I celebrated in my heart for another miracle that I felt I was granted. I named the baby after Sister Williams whose prayers had meant so much. Alice Faye Hein had been born on May 25, 1953 and she was feisty.

When Alice was eight days old the kids and I were at the table eating lunch when we were interrupted by a commotion at the front door. Mrs. Barton was banging on the door and shouting, "Your house is on fire! Flames are coming out of the roof! Get out! Hurry! I'll get the fire department!" She ran off.

Hugo was working out of town; my thoughts went flying.

"Joyce, get the baby out!"

"Lourene, get the little kids out and keep them together!"

"Son and Butch, get some water up there!"

We all scattered. The sewing machine which had helped me clothe the family and earn money for us, was like my best friend; it was the first thing I went for. I started dragging it out the door.

Son and Butch worked with buckets and pans. Son had the fire totally put out before the fire department arrived. We were so blessed. When Hugo came home he had to patch the roof, but we had no major damage and we lost nothing, personally. I'm sure I gained a few gray hairs.

When Alice was three months old we moved to a bigger and better house. The Schulens place was on Avenue E. It had a long porch across the front. We had four bedrooms here because the living room doubled as a bedroom.

When we had moved to Somerville Joyce had gotten a job at the Santa Fe Café and she worked evenings after school and on Saturday and Sunday. She was hoping to stay out of the cotton patch. (The café changed from Santa Fe Café to Sloan's to Ottmer's to Dishers as it was bought and sold three times.) Joyce was very witty and people liked to be around her. Teachers and students admired her.

She had heard of a young soldier whose letters written home about the Korean War had been printed in the Somerville paper. He had signed up for two years of military service, but Uncle Sam had added a third year when the U.S. entered the war. Since moving to Somerville Joyce had seen him around because he often sang for school functions. She finally met Billy Balke when she and five friends went to Jack's Place after a Friday night football game. Some students always met at Jack's for dancing after the games. Billy, being older, was not a part of the high school dance group.

Seated at the bar, he noticed her big smile from afar; he thought he had seen her around too. A mutual friend introduced them and the sparks started flying almost immediately. They both loved to dance and after a first date to an A&M football game, they spent most Saturday nights dancing at the Goldstar, Bill Ritter's place, in Caldwell.

We were excited when Joyce was selected to represent the Junior class at the high school Maifest. She wore the beautiful pale green prom dress that I had made for her (I knew I needed that sewing machine). The bodice fit perfectly and the skirt was full with lots of gathers. The dress didn't really matter, it was her big smile that captured everyone. Dorothy and LaVerne sent her ballerina style shoes to complete the outfit.

Billy asked Joyce to marry him that summer. He had gotten a job in Texas City right after coming home from the Korean War, always returning to Somerville for the weekends, and he wanted her to be with him.

Joyce's wedding was in early June. I gave birth to my eleventh child 19 days later (unbelievable, **me** with 11 children). Sarah Jean was born on June 23, 1955. Like Alice, Sarah was also born in Sarah B. Milroy Hospital in Brenham. When I had gotten pregnant with her I felt that I just could not go on. Hugo wasn't working again. I sewed, washed, ironed, and quilted. I don't know how many quilts I did for $3.00 a quilt. Minimum wage went to $1.00 an hour. I was so underpaid! I did everything I could to help care for the family. We could never qualify for welfare because Hugo was not disabled, only out of a job a lot.

I did every job I could. Being in town and living closer to people allowed me to also clean houses for money. Sarah was a beautiful, healthy baby and her birth was not complicated; I did go on even though people gossiped about us. We really did have too many kids for our income, but they were our blessing.

When Joyce got married that meant that all four of the older girls were now married. They were building their own lives, their own families, but they were still Hugo's little girls. He had gotten a job as a carpenter, building homes in Houston and had rented a room down there for a while. His brother Leo was a builder and Raymond had a drywall company. We got a telephone so Hugo could keep in touch with us. He also bought a car, a Chevrolet. (I was assistant mechanic and memorized the parts on that vehicle too.)

When that job ended and he came home, he started calling the girls, often. All those calls were long distance calls which cost higher rates. I cautioned him about the phone bill, but he missed the girls. They had been his bubbly little work crew for so long.

"You know what, Nora Mae? If I want to check on the girls, I'll check on the girls."

And he did. We couldn't pay the phone bill so our service was disconnected.

Before Sarah was a month old, Alice, who was a two year old bundle of energy (I often told Alice that I would have become rich if I could have bottled her energy and sold it), slipped away from me and out the back door. I missed her almost immediately and through the screen door could see her standing on the top step; there was no porch there. This house was built on a slightly sloping piece of property. In the front there were three steps up to the porch, but in the back, there were five steps and they were narrow across and steep. She was on the top step, standing just to the left of the door. I opened the door just enough so I could reach around to grab her, but as I opened the door she danced back toward it. The door knocked her off the steps to the ground with her head banging as she landed. Being overwhelmed with anxiety, I sank to my knees beside her. She was dazed, but finally sat up alone. She cried a long time and I knew something was wrong.

The doctor couldn't help us. Alice had learned to talk at an early age, and she talked a lot. Now she could only stutter. There were no more happy giggles; she stuttered and then she cried out of her frustration. It was very agonizing as a parent, not being able to help fix the problem. We went to church and I asked Sister Williams to pray for her. She put a small amount of prayer oil on her finger, touched Alice's forehead, and prayed. A miracle happened! Alice began to speak normally. Hugo often laughed and said, "She has been talking ever since." Her talking did seem pretty nonstop at times. Tillman would try without success to quiet her,

"Quieten down; they don't need to hear you two blocks over!"

Without a doubt, Jesus had healed her. The right kind of noise can make such a difference in a home.

1955 was a special year for another reason: Jonas Salk reported the success of what he called, his anti-polio vaccine. That vaccine was going to be really important to my family.

1956 was a hard year for my Mama as "Old Man" Brinkmann died. It wasn't too long and Mama and two of my half-sisters sold the farm and moved closer to Caldwell. We helped them move.

I loved flowers and had purple petunias growing by the side of the house. A trail went around the house; the flowers grew next to the house along the trail. As Alice and Sarah grew, they were always picking my petunia blooms and turning them upside down to be miniature ladies with flowing skirts. They used four inch long sticks for their guys. I kept telling them not to pick all my flowers, but it was hopeless; they thought the purple blooms looked like such gorgeous flowing dresses.

My flowers weren't the only thing they enjoyed. They also got into Lourene's make-up which she had bought with her own money. They were lipsticked to the hilt and the lipstick tube was mostly ruined.

"You just wait, you little brats! When I get married I'm going to bring my kids to your house and let them mess up your stuff. You just wait."

They were ashamed and repentant for the moment.

Virginia and Tillman got the idea that they wanted to try to fly. Well, Superman did it, you know. They planned to jump off the roof of the smokehouse, landing behind it. They decided to use my umbrella as sort of a parachute just in case they needed air support. Tillman went first and landed well.

"It's great! Your turn!"

As Virginia floated down the umbrella turned inside out. Now they were worried about having ruined my umbrella, so jumped again without it. They invited Alice to jump, "Come on! It's fun!"

Alice was a little younger and less of a risk taker. She decided to check out the landing area before she leaped. There was a pile of boards to one side. She stepped up on the pile which flattened as a nail went all the way through her foot. She never made it to the roof; the flight experiments were done. The older kids told me that Nellene had tried the same thing from the much taller barn on Kystenik's place. Her cape was a sheet and she knocked the wind out of herself as she landed, scaring them all. My – I had a bunch of super heroes!

The Schulens smokehouse backed up to the chicken pen which had a heavy gate; it seemed really heavy to the kids. Alice would follow the older kids out there, but she was afraid of the chickens, especially the rooster. If I told her to gather the eggs, she would run in, lickety split (I hope you've heard that expression before); she'd get the eggs, and sprint to the gate. Because she ran, the chickens would always be chasing her on the way out. One day I heard her crying and screaming,

"Mama! Mama!"

I ran out the back door.

She was crying big tears and shouting, "Mama! Mama! The chicken got its head caught in the gate! The chicken got its head caught in the gate!"

Sure enough, the gate had slammed right on the chicken's neck as Alice rushed out. The chicken which was suspended in the air was scared, but okay; I carefully opened the gate, releasing her from the strangle. She shook herself and ran off.

Tillman was always teasing his younger sisters about something. The bathroom had a small window above the bathtub. It was too high up for anyone to see in, but was big enough to let in the light during the day. When the youngest girls would take a bath Tillman would frighten them to tears. He would stand outside below that window and say loudly,

"Wooly Bully's gonna' get you!

"Wooly Bully's gonna' get you!"

He couldn't reach the window, but he would hold my mop upside down and move the head of the mop up and down by the window.

"Wooly Bully's gonna' get you!"

In the early evening light the girls could see the mop head with the strings cascading down like hair. They would begin to scream which would encourage him and he would move the mop head more. "Wooly Bully's gonna' get you!"

I always rushed in to save the day when they began to scream. I explained to them about the mop. I punished Tillman and later showed the girls the mop and told them what he had been doing. That didn't matter, every time he pulled the "Wooly Bully" stunt they were scared beyond reason. He got a good laugh out of it even though he knew he would get in trouble. He enjoyed aggravating them.

One day he cockily told them, "If I put a watermelon seed into my ear, it will come out in my mouth! Watch!"

He put a seed in his ear, made a face or two showing concentration, then opened his mouth to show ...... a watermelon seed.

"Nuh uh! That's not true," Virginia yelled.

"Yes, it is. Watch closely."

He put a watermelon seed in his ear again, removing it as he turned his head so they couldn't see, and then he opened his mouth. Again there was a watermelon seed in his mouth.

"Do you see it?"

Sarah, the youngest, said, "You had that in there to start with." But it almost sounded like a question.

"No, look." Tillman opened his mouth, keeping the watermelon seed under his tongue, "See. My mouth is empty."

He repeated the trick, discreetly moving the seed from under his tongue. "Behold, now you see the seed has reached my mouth."

Virginia and Alice could see that Sarah was captured. They joined in the tease.

"Isn't it amazing?"

Sarah, being the inquisitive little thing that she was, had to figure out how this worked.

About twenty minutes later, she came to me crying, holding her ear.

"It won't go through. It won't go through."

She had shoved a watermelon seed so far into her ear that I could see I could not get it out.

"Oh! These kids!" (Sometimes it was like a three ring circus.)

I had to take her to Dr. Pazdral. Sarah was so frightened that it took three adults to hold her down while Dr. Pazdral got that watermelon seed out.

The joys of parenting can be complicated. You have to be a just judge. If you have kids, good luck!

Chapter 11

A Major Miracle

On Easter week-end the older kids came home to visit. We were a large group departing church. Hugo left in his vehicle with several of our kids and I rode with one of the girls. To our dismay, when we got home we discovered that neither of us had gotten Alice.

"I thought she was with you!"

"I thought you got her! I was carrying Sarah!"

She had fallen asleep on the pew so we didn't disturb her as we greeted church friends after the service. We had left her there! I needed to get lunch spread for our large family group so I sent Son back on his bicycle to get her. He rode like the wind and found her still asleep on the pew. Not knowing that we had left her, she wasn't frightened. Son awakened her and they mounted up. She held tightly to him on the ride to the house. I guess leaving one kid out of eleven over the years was not too bad of a record, but still … Alice was the same kid who as a three-week old baby got dragged across the floor by her three year old sister! Hmmm.

Joyce and Billy gave us an electric cook stove which made my kitchen seem, oh, so modern. Using an electric stove instead of a wood burning one really changed my routine and made my life much easier.

Son, Butch, and Lourene were actively involved in high school and all were working. Lourene worked as a soda jerk at Community Drug after school and at Bill Buerger's Grocery Store on Saturday. She had become a good seamstress, learning to sew in Home Economics class. She made corduroy coats with linings for her little sisters. Son and Butch worked as helpers on local farms. I had thought when we moved to Somerville our cotton picking days would be over, but my teens sometimes joined other youth in town picking cotton on nearby farms.

Hugo, now working in College Station, was almost home one day when a vehicle ran into his. His Chevrolet was a total loss and he had to get it towed home. He was banged up pretty badly and the kids were scared by the appearance of his scratches, but he was okay. Now he would have to catch a ride to work (28 miles away) and I was back to walking to the grocery store (a few small town blocks away).

The younger kids walked with me to town and Lourene stayed home. We were all carrying groceries on the way home. When we were almost to our yard which was fenced in we could hear Lourene hollering, "Stop! Don't come!

There's a mad dog by our fence." We could see a large brown dog just outside the fence.

A mad dog was a dog that had rabies. If you could see his mouth foaming he was already in bad shape.

We scurried up on our next door neighbor's porch. Mrs. Farris had also seen the dog. She telephoned the deputy sheriff who did come and shoot the dog as it ran toward him. As he handled the dead dog, we walked quickly home to get our groceries put away. The tests proved that that dog did have rabies.

Butch did not like to study and didn't ever study much. He was often accused of having a photographic memory and did well on rote memory stuff. When studies required more application he was disinterested. He turned sixteen in January of 1957 and got a job at the Phillips 66 service station in town. When school started that fall he decided that he was not going back. He worked and saved money, soon buying a car, a 1953 red Chevrolet convertible with a white top. He loved his car and kept it shining. He gave all Lourene's friends rides to the dances and made sure they all had a ride home. He was like a big brother to them.

Son was more serious about school, completing all required courses even though he worked at Lewis' Texaco Station during the school term. During the summer he worked at Crow's Ranch not far from town. He graduated from high school in 1958 and Hugo, who had developed into a skilled carpenter, helped him get a job with the Skravanek

Building Company. Son later bought himself a convertible too. His was a black 1951 Ford with a white top.

Lourene learned to play piano and became part of a three way rotation for playing piano at church. Her friend Betty Jo played piano also. Sister Williams' oldest son had gotten married and his wife Marie was the third person in the rotation. They spent lots of hours playing and singing.

Tillman and the little girls came in laughing one afternoon. They had decided to play in Hugo's wrecked Chevrolet and were delighted to find ... hard candy! Hugo had stopped to get candy for them on his way home the fateful day of the wreck. The jerking of the wreck and then the towing had caused the candy to be scattered. Some had gotten under the seats and they really enjoyed the surprise when they found it this day.

One of the neighbors had left-over birthday cake and came to give it to us. When she described the delicious red velvet cake my mouth was watering. She figured our crew would certainly enjoy it. As soon as she left, with anticipation I called the kids in. I opened the foil to reveal a cake that was moving; it was full of ants! We had to throw it out as quickly as we could. We laughed a long while about that. I guess the chickens liked it.

It was not a laughing matter when in July of 1958 Tillman suddenly became ill. He had a headache, fever, and vomiting for about twenty-four hours. The next day he seemed okay, but had no appetite. The next morning he could not stand. When he tried to get out of bed, he wilted to the floor screaming in severe pain, "Mama! Mama!"

I couldn't help him. I thought that maybe he was just weak from not eating. I propped him up on the bed and Lourene desperately tried to feed him, but he couldn't eat. We took him to Dr. Pazdral who made the frightening diagnosis – Tillman had polio. Polio! The dreaded worst disease of the Post War Era had attacked him. The doctor questioned us extensively and decided that he must have been exposed to the virus at a summer camp that he had attended in June. Other than that trip he had pretty much been at home.

Polio is highly contagious at certain stages and can be spread by as little as a sneeze on someone's food or by sharing a bite of food with saliva on it with someone. It attacks the digestive tract first. We had nine people living in our home, so vaccinating them was crucial. Tillman had to be taken to Houston for treatment.

The fortunate thing for us was that doctors had been studying polio for a long time. Franklin Delano Roosevelt who did become the 31st President of the United States was struck with polio in 1921. He founded the March of Dimes Foundation to develop a vaccine in 1938. He made a radio announcement in which he asked all listeners to send in a dime and the White House received 2,680,000 letters within days.

In 1947 Dr. Jonas Salk, who had been born to Jewish parents in 1914, joined the research team at the University of

Pittsburgh School of medicine. 1952 brought the worst epidemic in US history with 3,145 dying of polio and 21,269 people left with mild to disabling paralysis. Salk was devoted to finding a vaccine; he worked 16 hours a day, 7 days a week, for years. By 1955 sixty-seven million dollars had been given to combat polio. Most researchers experimented using live virus, but Salk used a safer killed virus. When news of his vaccine success was made public he was labeled a miracle worker. To everyone's surprise he did not show interest in personal gain. When asked if he would patent his vaccine he replied, "There is no patent. Could you patent the sun?" Wikipedia records that the worth of a patent was calculated to have been seven billion dollars.

Much research had also been done in treating polio patients. Our older girls came to make sure all of us got where we needed to be. Some were taken to Galveston to be vaccinated; they received polio shots in the buttocks. Tillman was taken to Hedgecroft Comprehensive Rehabilitation Center in Houston. The first days were dark, bleak days for him. At church our friends prayed that he would survive.

I initially stayed at the hospital with him. It was explained to me that Tillman's recovery was going to be a long process with no guarantees. When Hugo came to visit bringing the younger girls they were dirty and their hair was disheveled. I was embarrassed. They were not filthy, but I could see they needed my touch. LaVerne accepted the monumental task of picking up Till's clothes every week, washing them, ironing his shirts, and then taking them back. I made a decision to go home. Sometimes in life you have to make tough decisions. Sometimes none of your options are good, but you still have to choose. I decided to go home.

It became evident that Till was going to survive; he graduated to a wheelchair. At church we began to pray that he would walk again. It was easy for me to ask for a miracle. Sister Williams just expected them. Hugo and I had taken the family on the train to Houston earlier that year. Some of us went to hear Evangelist Oral Roberts who was holding a crusade at the Sam Houston Coliseum. Thousands of people filled the arena. The music team was playing "Expect a Miracle Every Day." In this atmosphere we saw thousands of people healed as Oral Roberts prayed for them. Some in wheelchairs got up and walked. Some threw off their leg braces. Those are things one doesn't forget. I could definitely pray for my own son.

After a while Tillman was allowed to leave with his wheelchair on the week-end. LaVerne sometimes took him to her house for visits and her husband Guno Chollett enjoyed having him around. Hugo occasionally took off early on Friday and made trips to visit Till on week-ends.

Hedgecroft provided Tillman some very memorable experiences. He met two dogs who were TV/movie stars: Rin Tin Tin, a German shepherd and Lassie, a collie. As time passed Till began to reach out to the younger kids. He organized wheelchair races to help keep moral high. The recreational director and the nurses could see this young boy was becoming a role model. During the course of his stay Tillman looked after 7 or 8 younger boys. Toward the end of his stay the *Houston Chronicle* ran an article on this remarkable eleven year old kid, my kid.

Joyce and Billy picked him up twice and brought him to Somerville for week-end visits. LaVerne also brought him home a few times. They would pack and unpack the wheelchair. Sarah liked to stand on the back of it and ride. I had to watch her.

The last of Till's physical therapy was swimming. My friends and I were praying every time we went to church. The hospital staff was working with him every day. More than nine months from the time he entered the Rehabilitation Center he was released. When LaVerne brought him home, he was walking. I watched with tears running down my face. God is good. Till had a slight limp, but, oh, my! He was walking!

He had brought home a pair of stilts and he could walk on those too! He also brought a parakeet. He had missed almost a full year of school and his schoolmates were very excited to have him back. They had seen the newspaper article about him; he had a little bit of a celebrity status his first week home, but soon he was back in routine. The doctors encouraged me to have him join the marching band. He needed some type of consistent exercise; Somerville had no public swimming pool.

The younger girls said that I always treated Tillman differently after he came home. I thought I was being fair, but they said he hardly seemed to get in trouble anymore. Once you've had a child walk to the brink of death and come back, I guess you view them differently. After pleading with God so long, you become more cautious about how you treat your miracle kid. I didn't think I gave him preferential treatment, but the younger girls said I did.

When school started in the fall of 1959, I accompanied the kids to the schoolhouse. Alice was starting first grade and I wasn't sure about Tillman's placement. Although he had missed almost all of fifth grade, they decided to put him in sixth grade. It was the right thing to do because although his book education that year had been lacking, he had gained leaps and bounds of knowledge.

For Christmas that year Joyce and Billy gave Alice and Sarah beautiful baby dolls with soft hair. Not long after, Tillman and Virginia, for some unknown reason, cut both dolls' wonderful hair off – like – bald sort of haircuts! When Alice and Sarah cried they tried to cover up their sin by gluing the hair back so I wouldn't see what they'd done. The only problem was that they used the glue that Tillman had for his airplane models. It was cement glue that turned a dark silvery gray color when it dried. The dolls now had horrible shiny gray spots all over their heads. The doll hair didn't stick to it much either. It was much worse than bald would have been! Alice and Sarah played with them anyway. I guess things were back to normal – Tillman aggravating his little sisters again.

Hugo continued to do construction work in Bryan and College Station, Texas for Skravanek Builders. Son got a job with the Texas Agricultural Experiment Station and traded in his convertible for another car.

In June of 1960 Maddox Furniture Manufacturing Company of Brenham opened a second location in Somerville and they were hiring seamstresses. I prayed that I would get a job. I promised God that if he would help me get a job I would put $1.00 in the offering every week. (I have doubled that again and again and again.)

I did get the job and had to purchase a pair of scissors that was twelve inches long and heavy. The thread spools we used were 6.5 inches tall. The sewing machines were electric and they were powerful; definitely different than my foot pedal one, but I was determined that I could handle it. Floy Mae Moravek got a job as cutter (cutters cut the fabric) and became the head cutter at Somerville, also keeping the time. I was a bit slow on that new sewing machine and I am sure she regretted having to tell me to go faster. My job was to sew cushions and a certain quota was expected. If the number was short it was Floy Mae's job to make sure we caught up. She was younger than most of us so that was a challenge for her. Sometimes I would be intently trying to go faster with the cumbersome fabric and to ease the stress I would begin to sing. The machines were loud so I was always surprised when I realized the other girls could hear me singing.

"Nora Mae's singing again," someone would say as I crooned, "Amazing Grace, how sweet the sound, that saved a wretch like me!" I loved John Newton's song and it poured from me with rhythm.

"Yes. She's got us rockin' and a rollin' again!" Floy Mae would laughingly comment.

I just kept singing. I was determined to keep up, "I can do this. I can do this."

In order for me to work I had to arrange childcare for Sarah who was five years old, not yet old enough to go to school (we had no kindergarten in Somerville ISD at that time). In the fall when the other kids went back to school I hired someone to babysit Sarah. When I went to work it was too early in the morning for Sarah to go so the kids walked her to the babysitter's house a bit later, and then walked back to the school. Floy Mae picked me up for work and I was having a time getting everything done in the mornings. I had to get up really early to get the bread ready and baked before I left. I was usually trying to hurry it out of the oven when Floy Mae honked out front. She was always scolding me for being late; after all, she was the time keeper and we had to punch the clock! I felt like I was always running out the door.

Floy Mae gave me a ride to work, but I usually walked to get groceries and to church. All this walking had to be good for us, I am sure. If we look we can find blessings all around us – working in a factory exposed me to things I had not been able to reach for before. I was eventually able to purchase medical insurance for the family. I also had a fifteen minute break built in every morning and every afternoon; that was different!

The church Youth Group kept the teen-agers busy and me too, as I taught the Youth Sunday School class. Our church had monthly youth rallies with Sister Stork's church. Son first met Dolores Catlin at one of the rallies. She played piano at Sister Stork's church. On Sunday mornings after playing at her church, she would drive to the Lutheran church to play organ for them. What a great gal she was! She and Hugo Junior (Son!) got married in December of 1960.

When Butch went into the United States Army in January (he volunteered for the draft), my insurance man encouraged us to buy life insurance on him so I did. Wow! Our first two boys were gone from home. That took some adjusting to. Both the boys cars were gone and occasional rides were no longer possible. There were only five kids at home now so Alice, second grade, and Sarah, age 5, were able to inherit a bed to sleep in. They had slept with me as babies and then graduated to a pallet on the floor. Every morning they rolled up their pallet and slipped it under my bed. At night they rolled it out again. They were as happy as two little larks and never even thought about it; I was the one who was excited to let them move into the room that Son and Butch had occupied.

Chapter 12

Muddy Water

This is one of the most painful parts of my journey because I had to step into waters that I did not want to go into and they were muddy waters, so muddy that I couldn't see where I needed to step. But there was no waiting for me to prepare myself – I had to step in just as I was and find my way to the other side. And I was not alone as when I was young, this time I had a train of children following me, trying to find their steps too.

Psychologists tell us that a major life change, for instance, a death or a child leaving home, gaining a new family member, a wife beginning or stopping work (the list is long), can cause tremendous emotional and mental stresses as people adjust. Two or more major life changes within the same year can cause serious problems. Dr. Thomas Holmes and his associates developed a rating scale, the Social Readjustment Rating Scale (SRRS), which coordinates life changes (both good and bad changes cause stress) with illness. Their theory is that any accumulation of 200 to 299 points within one year gives a person a 50% chance of illness. More than 300 points in a year raises the percent of illness to 80%.[6] Having faced Tillman's illness, 2 sons leaving home, changes in his job, no vehicle, on top of the responsibility of providing for his large household, Hugo had more than 200 points on the SRRS two years in a row.

All this was affecting him. Another factor that affected him was that he had always been extremely jealous of me; and then there was the alcohol factor. A booklet published by Gospel Publishing House of Springfield, Missouri in 2002 states that "even small amounts of alcohol can affect a person's ability to make proper judgments and to safely operate anything mechanical, including bicycles and cars; drinking makes accidents more likely. Alcohol can also put people in a fighting mood..."

Hugo drank wine off and on; it always affected his judgment and his mood. He became very mean when he drank alcohol. A couple of my daughters have dealt with hyperglycemia and know how sudden changes in blood sugar levels can affect a person's thinking. Perhaps spiking the sugar levels was what the wine did to affect Hugo so profoundly. Whatever it was, I hated alcohol. Hugo more than once promised me that he wouldn't drink anymore and, his promise would sometimes last for years. I'm not sure if an old friend came along or a really good paycheck put him in a celebrating mood, but in February of 1961 he began to drink wine again. He could never fool me, I could immediately recognize the effect of even one drink; he couldn't stop with one. We argued in the evening a few nights in a row.

When he drank alcohol it seemed like he had a jealous demon to the extent that it made no sense. One night as the argument escalated he hit me on the face, jarring my head, and leaving a full handprint visible to the kids. One of them immediately hit him back and he wilted. I knew this was wrong; you can't have a kid hitting their father. We weren't way out in the country anymore, we were in town and I could ask for help. I had to make a decision. I was a Sunday School teacher, my kids were deeply involved in activities at school and church, and this was a small town.

So, Nora Mae, what are you going to do?

I decided to risk the little status we had achieved and reach out to get help for him. I used a neighbor's phone and called the deputy sheriff. After I took that first difficult step, Hugo decided that he would go for the treatment they recommended. He was taken to Austin State Hospital in Austin, Texas which is run by the Texas Department of Mental Health. Dr. Thomas "Tom" Turner came to the Austin State Hospital Neuropsychiatry department in 1961. They were using some traditional and some controversial treatments at the time. Hugo would be there for about seven months. Every time I went to church my friends and I prayed for him. With him gone, our family budget imploded; it was inevitable. I had to ask my older kids for help just to get by.

When Sarah's caretaker was ill, Sarah, who was five years old, had to go to school with Alice. I didn't have a choice, I had to go to work. Alice took Sarah to class with her and had Sarah share her desk. Sarah tried to be inconspicuous as she behaved perfectly. The school never questioned it. They knew it was better for Sarah to be there than for my kids to have to stay home with her and Sarah didn't mind; she found it all very interesting. (Lyndon Baines Johnson who became 35th President of the United States felt that sitting in a classroom as a five year-old helped him so much he wanted it available for all, thus he later started Project Head Start.) During one two week period Sarah had to accompany Alice to school every day. They were doing school pictures during that time and that's how Sarah became the only one of my bunch who has her five year-old school picture. She just followed Alice.

Butch visited home in the middle of March; he was so handsome in uniform. Also in March, Joyce and Billy took me to visit Hugo. On that first visit he was not doing well. It affected me; I felt like I wanted to throw up. Have you ever felt so for someone you love? You can't reach them. You can't make it better. You don't even know what to do. (The best first aid kit has no instructions for this.) It was a bad feeling, but somehow I knew that I had done the right thing. I felt God's reassurance – the warmth of His presence. I knew His grace would be sufficient. Like Corrie Ten Boom wrote about her prayer time in the German concentration camp, God's presence was "heaven in the midst of hell."

I had asked my neighbor Mrs. Rhodes to keep an eye on the kids during that first visit to Austin. Wouldn't you know it? The kids were running and playing and Sarah stepped on a coffee can with a sharp metal edge, cutting her foot. She saw blood and began screaming hysterically. Mrs. Rhodes came and cleaned and bandaged the wound which eventually left a scar.

We took the kids with us the next time we visited. The sidewalk we took from the parking area was beside a chain link fence which surrounded a courtyard. Patients were allowed to enjoy the outdoors. The fence kept them safe. As we walked down the sidewalk one older man came over to the fence tremendously scaring the girls as he kept trying to reach them through the fence, and he was calling, "Little girl, come here. Little girl, come here." He followed us along the fence.

"Just keep walking," I ordered and was relieved when we reached the door. We had a good visit with Hugo that day.

Lourene graduated high school in May of 1961. By the end of the summer she had moved to Houston and found a job. She began sending money for Virginia and Alice to have piano lessons; she wanted someone to be able to take her place at the church piano.

The Berlin crisis began in June. Financially I was scratching the bottom of the barrel. In July Butch offered to get out of the army so he could come back and work to help the family. He instructed me to get four notarized letters and get him out if I needed to. He had witnessed a young man try to go AWOL and one try to commit suicide. He wrote that his army pay was $78 a month with them taking half of it back to pay for wall and foot locker expenses, and other expenses. Even trying to be frugal, he usually had no money left over. He did send me a little cash, but I did not make him get out.

In July President Kennedy called up 150,000 reservists and National Guardsmen to active duty because tensions with the Soviets in Berlin were high. On August 13, the Soviets sealed off the West zone of Berlin with a barbed wire fence constructed overnight to stop the citizens of East Berlin from defecting to the West. West Berlin citizens could not cross even to see relatives (2 years later, in December of 1963, Christmas visits were allowed).

LaVerne and her two kids took us on another trip to visit Hugo at the hospital in Austin. We could hear patients screaming as we walked past one of the buildings which gave us an eerie feeling. The screaming continued and the kids wanted to go back and wait in the car, and we let them. Can you imagine that? It was safe enough for us to let them wait in the car. Hugo was doing much better. We retrieved the kids to visit him too.

In September Butch, now that he was grown everyone was starting to call him Henry, was moved to North Carolina and was awaiting deployment to Germany. Hugo came home the same month.

We could immediately tell that he was better; we were so blessed. Many people are helped by that type of treatment, but not everyone recovers. We were fortunate: Hugo survived the treatments and they helped him. We had made it safely through the muddy waters.

It was a slow process, but our home life seemed to be returning to normal. Normal? How could it be normal, we only had 4 kids at home now. This wasn't normal, was it?

Tillman was becoming best friends with Dickie Meyer and Stevie Miller. Dickie had an electric train that they all loved and he only lived a street over from us. The boys who were all around age 13 were getting into the train world. They liked to go to the Somerville Depot to watch the trains come through. One interesting thing was the way the messages were passed if the train didn't stop. The station attendant would attach the message to a clip on a high pole near the depot. The engineer would grasp it as the train went slowly through the station. The conductor in the caboose would watch; if the engineer missed it on that first try, he would grasp it as he passed.

One night the boys decided that they wanted to go meet the 9:45 PM train. Hugo and I told Tillman that that was too late; he could not go. He didn't like it, but after arguing a bit he went on to his room. Virginia, Alice, and Sarah were all playing in Virginia's room which was next to Tillman's. They were laughing and carrying on and their squeals kept getting louder and louder. Suddenly I noticed the strangeness. Usually when they carried on I could hear Tillman yelling, "Shut up! Shut up!! Mama, make them shut up in there. I'm trying to sleep!"

Here it was – 10:00 PM, they were still laughing, and not a peep from Tillman. I went into Virginia's room.

"Do y'all hear Tillman?"

"No."

They quietened down. I went and opened the door to Tillman's room. There he was, under the covers, fast asleep.

It couldn't be, could it? His head was even covered up. It just couldn't be true; he always haggled his sisters.

I went and pulled back the cover and to my surprise there was a quilt rolled up the size of a person in the bed. Tillman was gone.

We knew exactly where he was. Hugo and I walked all the way down to the train station to confront him. He and Dickie were there; they had met the train and were still jabbering away.

Although we hated doing it, he got his rear end busted that night. The girls say that is the only spanking Tillman ever got after coming home from the hospital.

I don't know. I didn't keep records. I never liked to give spankings anyway and we only did it when we had to. For the most part my kids were good kids, mischievous maybe at times, but solidly good.

On September 11, 1961 Hurricane Carla, a category #4 hurricane hit the Galveston coast with a 22 foot storm surge, spawning 26 tornadoes and creating damage all the way to Dallas. The price tag for this hurricane was $325 million and on hurricane charts the damage was considered "extreme." Evacuation of Galveston had been done earlier. The devastating Galveston Hurricane of 1900 in which 8,000 people died had caused Galveston city government to raise the city 17 feet, build the sea wall and plan evacuations carefully. (Among those killed in the 1900 storm surge were Hugo's great aunt Pauline (Hein) Rosen, her husband Herman, and their children.) Because of the 1961 hurricane Somerville school was dismissed for 2 weeks as the Red Cross set up their headquarters at the school. Evacuees were staying in the Somerville gymnasium (you know, the WPA one that Hugo helped construct) and the Red Cross was providing meals there for them. We had lots of visitors at church during that time.

There was damage all around Somerville. Our house was intact, but a large cedar tree near the front porch, a tree that the kids had always enjoyed climbing, was snapped off near the ground; it fell across the porch roof crashing it in. The walls were not damaged. Virginia was sleeping next to that front wall. The noise was frightening, but her room was unscathed. The clean-up kept Hugo busy a few days. Then he began the monumental task of finding a job; he had been hospitalized, thus unemployed, for about seven months.

Shortly after Hurricane Carla we moved. Reverend Modschiedler was now pastoring in Michigan and he still owned his house in Somerville. Being so far away he wanted people that he could trust living in the house. He had been in our home many times when we had Vacation Bible School and Saturday "Sunday" School, so he offered to rent to us. The Modschiedler place was a wonderful, large house situated right in town and, you guessed it, right on state highway 36. This was the first time we had an indoor toilet in our bathroom. Yippee! It seemed that a room had been added to the back right side corner of the house at one time; it was not noticeable from the outside because the house had nice siding all the way around, but in the closet which backed up to the bathroom there was a double wall. The wall which was behind the hang-up clothes rod was made of white interlocking wooden siding. If you pulled one of the boards just right you could take out three of them in the middle of the wall and thus reveal a small area about 20 inches wide by 5 feet long. Intriguing! I wondered if any Germans or a ham radio had been hidden there during World War II when we had the internment camps in Texas. For a while we didn't even realize that the secret little room was there, but the kids found it. The large added-on room had its own door to the outside which added to the mystique.

This house had six large rooms, a bathroom, a utility room, a large front porch, and a smaller screened-in porch in the back. It was a great place with oleanders and crape myrtles in front and pecan trees in the enormous back yard. Modschiedler also owned the adjoining lot so the place took up almost half of the entire small town city block. It had a separate double garage and a chicken house with a nice chicken pen. This was our new home.

Maddox closed the Somerville furniture factory so my job moved to Brenham. Friends offered me the opportunity to ride in their carpool to work. There was no longer time for making bread in the mornings; I had to start buying bread. Hugo was having a hard time finding a job. Henry sent money home to us in April. All the kids were helping out along the way; I just remember Henry's specifically because I have always kept the thirty letters he wrote to me while he was serving in the army. He was now in Germany and they were crowded on the base.

The kids had to go to school in June and on Saturdays to make up for time lost during Hurricane Carla holidays. Lourene sent money to help them go to church camp when school ended.

Also in June of 1962 the concrete Berlin Wall was constructed 100 meters behind the barbed wire wall; the concrete wall was an average 11 feet 10 inches high and more than a foot wide. (The fourth generation wall constructed in 1975 was more than three feet wide in some places.) Between the two walls was the Death Strip where they planted landmines. Berlin was a 9 hour train ride from where Henry was stationed.

In July he wrote that the army base became so crowded the guys were standing in line for two hours on Saturday just to turn in laundry. From a distance he saw a friend from high school and wrote me to get the young man's address. It turned out the friend had been living five buildings down for months, but with their schedules they had not seen each other – one division would be out on maneuvers while the other was training in KP duty and working on tanks, etc.

Making top tank crew in the company, Henry got clearance for a 3 day expense paid trip to Berlin; he arrived in Berlin on July 11. He also visited the East Sector of Berlin which was occupied by Soviet troops and said it was unbelievable: there were no churches there at all, only remains. World War II had ended 17 years earlier, but still there were nice fronts on the buildings facing the streets, with bombed out hulls in the back. There were food lines and dirty, filthy stores in partially bombed out buildings which had only 2 or 3 items on the shelves. In stark contrast the West Sector of Berlin had stores which were well stocked "like in the states"; this was made possible by Allied air drops.

Berlin was one great city demonstrating two vastly different results of the same war. I pondered it; I determined, "I will not let the battles of my earthly journey leave me barren. I will not be an empty shell. Even if I am trampled I will allow the Spirit of God to drop life into me."

I had turned 46 that year and didn't know it then, but I was not even half way through my journey.

What did I say about being trampled?

**Nora Mae
with
Mama
(Nellie Mae Schafer Corley)**

**Nora Mae's
Father,
Ruel Hughes Corley**

Nora Mae Corley

The Brinkmann Family
(Nora and Charlie are not in the photo)

**Nora Mae, far right,
with Corley siblings
in 1984.**

**Nora Mae's brother,
Charlie Corley**

**1930 – Nora Mae (age 14) with Martha Zgabay,
Mary Proctezek, Mary Zgabay**

**March, 1932-Nora Mae (far right) with
(L to R) Irene Hein and Lillie Duncan**

**Hugo Hein and Nora Mae Corley
married on April 11, 1932.
Wedding picture was taken a
few months later.**

Nora Mae with Grandpa Schafer

My "Glamour" Girls – 1941
(L to R) LaVerne, Dorothy, Nellene, Joyce (in front)

"Glamour" Girls 1948
Nellene, Dorothy, Lourene, LaVerne, Joyce

1943-
Nora Mae (age 27), Hugo (age 38), Lourene (baby)
Girls L to R: Nellene, Joyce, LaVerne, Dorothy
Boys L to R: Butch, Son

1955-
Larry Rabey, Nora Mae, Nellene Marie

1955-
My Youngest Four:
Tillman, Virginia, Alice, Sarah

1959 – the Hein Family
Back Row (L to R)-Hugo, Son, Butch, Lourene, Tillman
Front Row-Nora Mae, Sarah, Dorothy, Alice, LaVerne,
Nellene, Virginia, Joyce

The Hein family in 1963

1966
Hugo and Nora Mae

1967
Nora Mae, Nellene Marie, Dorothy

1973
"Let's see…" with Alice

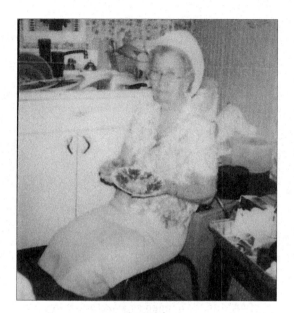

Cowgirl

Nora Mae waves from the
Somerville Community Action Team parade entry.

**1999
Nora Mae, fourth from left;
SAAM sends needed clothes to Arizona.**

SAAM HOUSE VOLUNTEERS sort and pack food items for the needy in Somerville. Some of the volunteers include Mickey Morris, Betty Johnson, Norma Davis, Nora Heine, Pat Zedlitz and Ella Mae Johnson. -- Tribune photo by Roy Sanders

**Somerville Area Assistance Ministry (SAAM) volunteers
shown in one of many newspaper clippings. Nora Mae
clipped this one from the *Burleson County Tribune*.**

Nora Mae's 80th birthday; with Hugo's siblings:
Leo Hein, Bessie Draehm, and Irene Tate.

1998
(L to R) – Sarah, Hugo Jr., Nora Mae, Alice, Lourene, Virginia,
Joyce, Dorothy, Tilman, and LaVerne

2006 SAAM Volunteers (L to R) front row: Anna Killough,
Nora Hein, Edna Spohn, Vivian Caldwell;
back row: Ruth Cummins, Tinka Murray, Ila Mae Brantley, Gloria
Sager, Mackie Meyer, Norma Davis, Lynda York

"LaVerne was my mainstay."
foreground – Virginia, Dolores (Hugo Jr.'s wife), Nora Mae, LaVerne

Chapter 13

Growing in Spirit

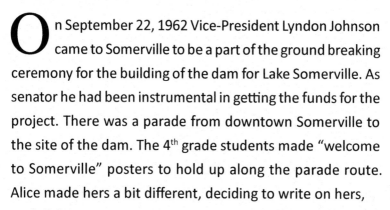

O n September 22, 1962 Vice-President Lyndon Johnson came to Somerville to be a part of the ground breaking ceremony for the building of the dam for Lake Somerville. As senator he had been instrumental in getting the funds for the project. There was a parade from downtown Somerville to the site of the dam. The 4th grade students made "welcome to Somerville" posters to hold up along the parade route. Alice made hers a bit different, deciding to write on hers,

"All the way
  with LBJ!"

The Vice-President noticed it and stopped to autograph her poster as he passed. Hugo attended the parade and was part of the group that was pictured with Vice-President Johnson in our local paper.

When work began on the large spillway that was built to allow water from the lake to overflow into Yegua Creek instead of flooding the town, Hugo was employed in the construction of it. When he got the job one of the first things he did was to give the kids ice cream money for lunch time at school.

I argued with him about it that day, "They are receiving free lunches. We need to pay our bills first. We really have a lot of catching up to do on our bills."

"Nora Mae, you know what? Here it is November and the kids haven't had ice cream money this school year. I want them to have it."

At the beginning of the school year a letter had been sent home inviting us to apply for free lunches for the kids which we did and we had been approved.

On the second day that Hugo sent ice cream money Alice's teacher said to her, "If you can afford to buy ice cream, you can afford to pay for your lunch."

We received a letter in the mail stating that the kids were being moved from "free lunch" to "reduced lunch" and we would now have to pay the price of an ice cream for each lunch. I don't think the government can move that quickly anymore. No red tape and no wasteful spending here! We never applied for free lunches again.

During these years we were growing in spirit; I was voted in as the teacher for the Adult Sunday School class and that sent me to studying a lot. The main thing I studied was the Bible; I think it is its own best reference book. After all, it is a collection of 66 books intertwined by God's spirit – Wow! Potent idea that is! I also studied other reference materials.

My lack of formal education bothered me, but I couldn't change the past and God had entrusted to me this teaching privilege. I had always loved learning so studying came natural to me; I immensely enjoyed sharing the things I learned.

And I totally loved singing! My younger kids did too. They were also singing with the church choir. We did not have a formal choir with try-outs; anyone who wanted to sing in the choir did. Each service everyone who wanted to participate in singing as a choir was invited to come to the front stage. Usually my whole family participated. Praising God in song allowed me to transcend any worry that tugged on my heart. For a few minutes nothing mattered, but God. Singing in the choir was therapy for my soul; I was reaching a place of internal refreshing and renewal – a fortification of my mind in preparation for whatever was up ahead.

Somewhere along the way I began to sing solos in church, not because I was such a great vocalist, but because God had been so good to me that I could meaningfully exalt Him.

The sermons were allowing my eyes to see the path God had for His children and how to walk it. Sister Williams had a great perspective on things. She said, "You can do a lot for God if you don't care who gets the credit."

She once told us that when someone had commented to her, "It's a useless ministry. You have the scum of the earth going to church over there;" she retorted, "You, my friend, forget that the scum floats on top!" She further elaborated,

"The scum of the milk is the best part." Then she laughed, "It's the cream!"

No, she didn't think we were scum; we had business people in our church as well as blue collar workers; all of us had been radically changed by the power of Jesus' blood. She felt that she had the best church in town, but she also knew that the Jesus chosen twelve were not the elite crowd, they were a motley crew. No one is too high in society; no one is too low. We are all in this together. Jesus uses all who come to him humble in spirit. And, "The scum floats on top!"

Every time I went to church it was like heaven piped into me nourishment for my spirit, enough for the current part of my journey, but I always wanted more of it, like Sister Williams sometimes said, "I was satisfied with an unsatisfied satisfaction." (I hope you can wrap your head around that.)

One of my friends from the work carpool, Louise Glass and her daughter Shirley, began to come to church too. Louise also found it to be a place of vital sustenance kindling inner joy.

Hugo's job on the Somerville Lake dam and spillway was fulfilling for him. He was enjoying the job (well, probably enjoying the paycheck, not so much the job) and his family. He took pleasure in commenting to the girls as they dressed for church on Sunday morning,

"How are my little bluebirds today?"

Or "How are my yellow birds this morning?" The girls enjoyed wearing the same color of dresses to church.

In January of 1963 Henry came home from the army. He went to Houston and stayed with LaVerne for a while. He worked with her husband and became a licensed plumber.

Hugo enjoyed the grandchildren as much as I did and the number was growing. Joyce gave birth to her third child on June 2, 1963. Robert Balke was my fourteenth grandchild. My first grandchild Linda Kay Chollett had been born when I was 36 years old, more than ten years earlier. Being a grand-mother was a rewarding feeling – once Linda Kay had arrived, grandkids seemed to arrive almost like popcorn – Lewis Ray (the first boy!), Arthur Nolan (Bo), Jimmie, Larry, Lloyd, Marleta, L.H. (Butch), Arthur Ernest (Junior), Linda, David Lee, Patricia, Cherie, and then Robert! Shortly after Robert was born, they discovered that Joyce had uterine cancer. This was 1963 and the treatment was radiation; the survival rate was very low so the prognosis was not good. Every time we went to church I asked for prayer for Joyce, my Joyce with her big smile and her ability to make everyone else smile too. None of us were smiling now as we sincerely asked God to heal her. She battled long and we kept praying.

It was a time of unrest in our nation. It was also a time of hope. In August Dr. Martin Luther King, Jr gave his "I have a dream" speech to 200,000 marchers in front of the Lincoln Memorial.

For her Burleson County Fair entry Virginia decided to make her Grandma Hein's little cookies that she called "tea cakes." We knew they were delicious so were thrilled when the judges agreed! Virginia won the blue ribbon! On November 2, 1963 Grandma Hein, Hugo's mom, died. What a loss we felt! Our hearts were aching.

1963 brought sorrow to more than just insignificant people like me. On Friday, November 22nd, our entire afternoon break crew went silent as the announcement came to us, "President Kennedy was shot in Dallas at 12:30 PM today as his motorcade passed through Dealey Plaza. He died at Parkland Hospital at 1:00 PM." Ahhhh! Did we hear it right? Some people were crying. I was numb. The whole nation was feeling heartache, but had to march forward.

Lyndon Johnson was sworn in as the 36th President, the first president from the south since Andrew Johnson followed Abraham Lincoln. In July of 1964 President Johnson was instrumental in passing the Civil Rights Act which made the segregation of blacks in public facilities illegal.

God was gracious to us. In the late summer Hugo noticed that the backyard grass was drying under the edge of the house which was on blocks and it had gotten really tall. He felt compelled to get the dead grass cleaned out so worked one entire day cutting grass and clearing all the tall stuff away from the house; the kids helped him; I was at work. The next day a fire started two houses down from us. It traveled quickly through wire fences from yard to yard and burned our dry back yard all the way up to the house before the fire department arrived. Hugo having cleaned all the tall grass from under the house the day before was the reason our house received no fire damage. God was very gracious. We had to be careful to not track black smudges into the house, but that was okay, we could be careful.

Tillman got a job delivering newspapers. His band teacher Mr. Schlabach helped him at first, then Till bought a green Chevrolet station wagon for hauling the papers. The girls sometimes helped him roll and tie them. Till drove to Dallas for the family to visit my sister Dorothy Jones, her husband, and their three girls. Dorothy and I wrote each other faithfully, but this was the first time my younger children had met her. She and I always seemed to hit it off when we were together, no matter how much time had elapsed in between visits.

Alma Norris contacted me. She was moving away from Somerville and was wondering if I would have room to store her daughter Betty Jo's piano. Betty Jo had moved to Temple a few years earlier so Alma had just kept the piano at her house, but she did not want to move it. Did I have room for the piano? You bet! It was like an answer to prayer! Virginia and Alice could now practice without having to walk to the church to do so. And practice they did! I loved the sounds of the music in the evening. I remembered long ago the kids laughing outside playing leap frog and how it comforted me at the end of a long day. This was much the same.

Virginia decided that piano was not her "cup of tea," but Alice practiced faithfully. Tillman would wail, "Please, please get her off that piano! Please!" Alice would immediately start playing Hugo's favorite song, "The Haven of Rest," and he never once told her to stop. It started sounding better after a while. I eventually bought the piano from Betty Jo.

Lyndon Johnson won the 1964 presidential election in a landslide vote. Early the next year, Tillman who turned 17, sold his green station wagon to us and got himself a newer car. He also started working at the local convenience store Handy Dandy, on week-ends.

It was a good thing Hugo got the car. One of the Lacina's relatives rode the bus from Houston to Somerville and then walked to our place (we were right on the highway) hoping she could visit with us a few days and then we could give her a ride to see her family. Of course we were happy to oblige. One of my best desserts was dewberry cobbler made from wild berries. At potlucks it was always a favorite so I made a cobbler for her while she was with us. The kids laughed when she refused to eat any of the cobbler saying, "Oh my, it looks bad. I probably should not. That purple color is very distraught. How old is it?" The hilt of insult, but seeing her expression I could hardly keep from laughing myself and the kids were happy to have more cobbler for themselves.

The kids also laughed when they went into the bathroom. It was a large room and I had a clothesline up in there for delicate things. We were amazed to see that she had washed all her money for some reason and had all the dollar bills pinned to the line to dry! We had heard her washing the coins; they were all lined up on the sink. She acted as if everyone always washed their money.

Now that we had a vehicle and "Old Man" Brinkmann was dead Mama was able to come and visit me. When Hugo and I brought her to our home for the first time we had been married for more than 30 years. She stayed with us for several days and we brought her more than once. She confided in us that a little bit of Mr. Brinkmann's strangeness still lingered around her house. Like him, my half-sisters were unusually afraid of germs and had begun to wash everything we touched during our visits to Mama's house. I didn't understand such actions, but I started making sure the kids were sitting in only one place when we visited. On a later visit to my home Mama again told me how my half-sister worked so hard scrubbing everything after each of our visits to her home. I eventually had the kids play outside when Hugo and I went in to visit. I am not sure if they were afraid of germs because Tillman had had polio or what the deal was. "Old Man" Brinkmann had always gone out the back door any time I had visited Mama when he was alive.

I felt like my family and I were wearing out the church prayer intercessors, but they didn't care; hallelujah, Joyce was declared cancer free! It was two years from when her treatments had started.

July brought joy and pain to our nation. Astronaut White walked in space and 50,000 troops were sent to Vietnam. Protests over the war began.

Integration of Somerville schools was implemented in the fall. In the mornings Alice walked across town with Sarah and then walked back to her school because the formerly black school was now the elementary school and Sarah was in fifth grade. The black students were intrigued by Alice's soft blonde hair and as the students walked from the junior high school building to the gym in groups, they would often come up behind her and stroke her hair again and again. She washed her hair every day and grew tired of it, but it was a long time before the different hair texture was no longer interesting to them.

Chapter 14

The Phoenix: Trampled, but Rising

Whe n war comes to us it never says, "Would you like death, destruction, and heartache?"

It only says, "Will you help me?"

We have to think of it as our sacrifice or our duty; if we think of it as our children's sacrifice we probably won't help very often. But there are principles that are worth sacrifice; as the old saying goes, war seems to be a necessary evil. Ecclesiastes 3:8 (KJV) tells us that there is a "time for war."

On November 1, 1963 President Kennedy had approved the coup that led to Diem's overthrow and death in Saigon, Vietnam. President Johnson and Congress tried to defend the new government, but the power vacuum there required more and more from us leading to full scale involvement. The realities of the Vietnam War began to bring division to our nation. It seemed to be a war that was unwinnable. Kids from every community were going off to war. It was as if a cloud was hanging over us.

It was the mercy of God that came to me on Mother's Day, 1966 as I was getting dressed for church. The warm presence of God entered my bedroom engulfing me and this thought entered my mind, "By Mother's Day next year one of your children will be dead." It floored me; it was like my heart tried to reject the message. I did not speak, but I stood still. Shortly, the presence lifted and I continued getting ready for church – I would still be teaching class this morning. That message stayed with me, but I told no one. I remembered how the scripture said that Mary, Jesus' mother, pondered things in her heart; I would ponder this.

In May Tillman graduated from high school. He did not have to go to war because polio had left him with such high insteps that he couldn't wear boots and he had a limp. Some of his friends did go.

Virginia got a job as a waitress at the City Café; she walked to work and we picked her up at 9:00 P.M. when she got off. Mama came that summer and stayed for a 3 day visit.

In late August Hugo's job at Lake Somerville wound down and he started working in housing construction in the Bryan – College Station area again. He began to arrive home from work with an argumentative attitude and my antennae went up. I looked in his car and found a wine bottle which I emptied and discarded. I found and emptied bottles several days in a row as Hugo's behavior became increasingly irrational. The girls even looked for wine bottles and dumped the ones they found hidden in the garage.

One Friday evening Hugo didn't accompany me and the girls as he usually did. We went to church and, unknown to us, he went to the City Café, causing a serious commotion with angry demands that made no sense and threatening a man who had recently asked Virginia to babysit his girls.

After church ended and most of the congregation had exited, the deputy Sheriff showed up, explaining everything to me and wanting me to go with him to get Hugo.

We easily found Hugo and he was again transported to the hospital in Austin. He was there for two weeks; the girls and I rode with Tillman to bring him home. He was released, doing fine, but was supposed to return for a check-up on Monday, October 10th. He said that he was not going back for the check-up; I said that he was.

Henry had been to Austin recently to take the exam for his plumber's license, which he passed. He agreed to take his dad there for the check-up so he came to Somerville the week-end of October 8th and 9th.

Hugo, the kids, and I were all asleep on Sunday night when Jimmie Schoppe and Mr. Westfall came banging on our front door. Virginia heard them first and went to the door.

"We need to speak to your mama and daddy."

She came to wake us, but we were already getting up. We went to the living room where they were waiting. Alice and Sarah were awake now too and they slipped in and were standing at the end of the couch. Jimmie Schoppe spoke slowly,

"We're sorry to bring bad news. We were returning from a trip to Houston and came upon a bad car wreck. Recognizing Henry's car, we stopped; he was dead in his vehicle which was against the pole near the creek."

Did he say, "dead"? I could hear him still talking, but my mind went back to Mother's Day and that warm presence of God which had said to me, "By Mother's Day next year one of your children will be dead." Here it was, plain as day, one of my children was dead. With all the emotional upheaval in our country and all I had just gone through with Hugo's relapse, I know it was God's mercy that had prepared me for this. It was not less painful, but I wasn't totally blindsided.

Jimmie Schoppe was still talking, "For some reason Henry drifted into the oncoming lane on the curve and ran head-on into another car. The other driver was killed also. Henry's car crashed then flew toward the creek, stopping against the pole. The other car was smaller and was squashed like a matchbox. The guy who had been riding with Henry said he was not hurt at all. He also said that they were headed to Petticoat Junction Truck Stop near Brenham to eat."

The talk continued. One of them said, "The last time I saw Henry, I told him to slow down." Someone said that a fog was settling in near the creek and might have affected Henry's vision …. I felt sort of foggy.

Henry was dead at age 24.

Jimmie Schoppe and Mr. Westfall took Hugo to use the phone at Jimmie's store, the Western Auto, so he could call

all the other kids. It was the middle of the night but they had to know that their brother Henry Roland Hein died in the early hours of October 10, 1966.

None of us wanted to believe it. Hugo Jr. called the Texas DPS to make sure it was true. Virginia went nuts with uncontrollable sorrow. That's what I wanted to do – scream, deny it, weep, but I had people to call and arrangements to think about which forced me to focus.

As the kids walked to school on Monday morning some boys came up behind Virginia saying,

"Some fool done got hisself killed last night."

That didn't help Virginia; none of the kids could concentrate on school. Dorothy, her husband Mack, and their boys came and when they returned home to Houston, they took Virginia with them for a couple of days, until the funeral.

Hugo and I visited Henry's car to see the wreckage and get items out of it. We collected the clothes that they had cut off Henry from the funeral home. Strange, but these things were therapeutic. It really did happen, he really was dead; denial seemed to be subsiding. And then we all saw him – in the coffin.

I had been trampled, squashed flat. I let God's spirit help me cope because I was determined to not become an empty shell. Sometimes I felt like a robot. Because our children are not supposed to die before we do, the pain surfaced again and again over the years, but God was faithful to comfort me as I always ran to him. I made myself sing again. As a glider rides on air currents I let him carry me along.

I wasn't the only one hurting; the entire family had to deal with grief. Hugo made strong personal commitments: he never returned to Austin for that check-up. In fact, he never drank alcohol again. Virginia worked through her grief in several ways. She wrote a poem about her brother and visited his grave as often as she could. Her friend Doris Rathjen had also experienced the loss of a brother – killed in a car wreck. They often visited Henry's grave together. And time did help.

Our nation was still in Vietnam, but by the end of 1966 we had successfully completed ten manned space missions. A sense of national pride was rising again in spite of the protests and the agony of the war.

The Lake Somerville project was finished in 1967. In the summer Dorothy and Mack invited Hugo and me to join their family on a road trip to California. Joyce invited the three girls who were still at home to stay at her house. We left Somerville at 8:05 AM Saturday morning, August 5, 1967. As we headed west we stopped in El Paso to walk over the river to Juarez, Mexico. It cost 2 cents to go over into Mexico and 1 cent to come back! The highlight of the trip was our two day visit to Nellene's house in Paramount, California which is very near Los Angeles.

Nellene had come to California in the 1950's and made it her home for many years. She pursued a career as an actress, but her only role was as an extra in a movie called *Violent Saturday* which was produced by 20th Century Fox in 1955. The movie starred Ernest Borgnine, Sylvia Sydney, Victor Mature, and Lee Marvin and was set in the years following World War II. It was filmed in Bisbee, Arizona. Nell was nineteen years old at the time of this movie. No, she didn't make the bigtime, but she tried. She was the only one of my kids who was in the movies at all! She did know a lot about the movie industry, but by now her movie pursuit had ended. She was now a married mother of six children.

On this trip we also visited many of our nation's outstanding sights – Garden of the Gods State Park, Petrified Forest National Park, the Painted Desert, Las Vegas lights, Hollywood, Long Beach (the Pacific Ocean), Universal City, Beverly Hills, the West Coast, San Francisco, Golden Gate Bridge, Lake Tahoe, the Great Salt Desert of Utah, Pike's Peak, Abilene. It was a wonderful trip! I recorded it all in a small journal: the cool, clear water streams; a wreck we saw; eating in a park with no shade trees; a dust storm surrounding our vehicle; acres of sunflowers; mucho mosquitoes in Arizona; some highways so bumpy that our luggage sang "wam wam;" even getting the radiator on Dorothy's car cleaned. And, "yes," we did drive up Pike's Peak; it took us about an hour to drive up to the peak where it was snowing. We traveled 5,498 miles and Hugo and I arrived back home at 8:05 PM on Tuesday, August 15!

Shortly after that trip Hugo and I bought a newer car, a beautiful red and white Chevrolet Impala.

In April of 1968, Martin Luther King, Jr. was assassinated in Memphis. The nation lost its most passionate spokesman for racial harmony, but his influence continued to shape our history.

Virginia got married in September of 1968. The dedication of Lake Somerville was held that same year and at Christmas we got a television from Hugo Jr. and Dolores. I had never watched much TV, but now, if I wanted to, I could. During the years that I worked at Maddox I always received a Christmas bonus on Christmas Eve. The amount was based on how many years you had been with the company. They took your years of service and multiplied by $10 and that was the amount you received. It was exciting for me. We always received our bonus on Christmas Eve and we got off at noon that day.

Hugo and the girls would pick me up from work and when we arrived home, the girls and I would hurry down to Strickland's Variety Store to get presents for the grandkids. I didn't have a lot to spend, but every grandkid would get something. It was such fun to pick the gift for each one. My children and their spouses would get a little bit of cash. After shopping for the grandkids we went by Benn's Grocery for Christmas food items. I also sneaked over to Western Auto to pay off and collect the lay-aways that I had there.

We arrived at the house with all the stuff and I started cooking pumpkin pies for the next day while the girls did all the wrapping, except for their gifts which Hugo had sneaked in; I always wrapped those after they went to bed. I also enjoyed giving gifts to my Sunday School class, but I usually did those a week earlier when we had the Christmas program at church. I loved being able to give them something even if it was small. Sending Christmas cards to friends and relatives was another thing I loved to do and I always displayed the cards I received. Keeping in touch with people was a highlight of the year for me. As I looked back to write about the sorrows and triumphs of the year I could always see God's hand in my life more clearly and my faith would grow stronger. It was a conscious decision to leave the old year behind and greet the new year with fresh hope.

Chapter 15

Two New Homes for Hugo

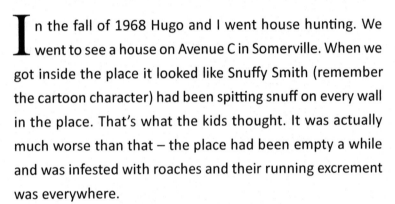

In the fall of 1968 Hugo and I went house hunting. We went to see a house on Avenue C in Somerville. When we got inside the place it looked like Snuffy Smith (remember the cartoon character) had been spitting snuff on every wall in the place. That's what the kids thought. It was actually much worse than that – the place had been empty a while and was infested with roaches and their running excrement was everywhere.

But Hugo and I had vision! We liked this house; we liked the location; we liked the price: we saw potential. We bought it; we bug bombed the place, scrubbed from top to bottom, and bug bombed again. Hugo had ideas for remodeling and my half-brother Hubert Brinkmann who was also a carpenter, helped him. They worked for months, putting up new paneling in the living room, the front parlor, and the bedrooms. We repainted all the doors and windows and the kitchen. They remodeled the entire bathroom, replacing every fixture and adding a linen closet. The kitchen got new cabinets and sink, paint, and linoleum.

In May of 1969 Virginia graduated high school; on July 20, Neil Armstrong and Buzz Aldrin walked on the moon; on Thanksgiving Day we moved into our "new" home! Hugo and I were off from work and some of the kids came to help us move. I cooked a turkey and one of the girls brought one too. We had a turkey at each house.

Our meal was a transitional one. We did sit to eat, but had our seconds while we worked. Everyone, except Sarah, that is; she spent most of the day in the rocking chair, rocking Tracie Vaughn, our newest grandbaby who had arrived on September 16 that year. She had been born in the hospital in Brenham so I was able to get over there from work and help welcome her to the world! I need to catch you up on our grandbabies. Since the last count we had now added three: Donald was born in 1964, Joel in 1966, and now Tracie, who was number 17, became the latest attraction. Tracie always had a special link with Sarah. We worked all day and got our stuff moved to the new place! We were excited. Our friends gave us a "house warming;" they were excited for us.

Having a car, Hugo and I became very involved driving the girls to church youth group rallies (in Hempstead and Waller, Texas), to play practice, to volleyball practice, etc. God was continually answering our prayers. The girls got a new male P.E. teacher one year who required them to purchase and wear extremely short gym suits. Notes were sent home on Friday asking for money to buy the gym suits. My girls always wore mid-thigh shorts for P.E. and their basketball and volleyball uniforms were short, but not like those gym suits! The girls said, "They are very short, Mom."

I'm thinking like, "We're not doing that."

We had church that night so I asked Sister Williams to pray with me about the situation. We prayed and on Monday when the girls went to gym class the new coach announced that he had changed his mind. No one would have to buy the gym suits; the modest shorts would be accepted. I never talked to anyone at the school about it; we prayed about it and God intervened. Maybe some other parent talked to them, I don't know; but I do know that our prayer was answered.

Sometimes I felt like my younger kids had more opportunities than the older ones. I almost felt guilty about it, but then I remembered that the older ones had some privileges that the younger ones missed out on. The only grandpa the younger ones had ever met was "Old Man" Brinkmann who hardly cared to even talk to them. The older ones had wonderful memories of their Grandpa Corley and their Great Grandpa Schafer. I had to think of it as embracing life each day and being thankful for the blessing each day brings, however large or small the blessing is.

The younger kids attended Somerville schools all their school days and were blessed with incredible teachers like Eunice Welch, Lillian Brinkman, Charles Sanders, George

Williford, Milt Jasek, Johnelle (Duewall) Kasprowicz, Robert Schlabach, Lois Broach, Lynda York, John Pinkerton, Howard Hitchcock, and Wilton Giesenschlag (Mr.G). They never switched school districts so their curriculum was very well aligned.

Our kids were on district winning ball teams. They were officers in FHA and FFA. Our family had a Vice-President of the Student Council, a Homecoming Queen, a Yegua Princess (equal to Miss Somerville High School), the third highest in graduating class, a Salutatorian (2nd highest in graduating class), and when Sarah graduated she was the Valedictorian (highest in her class). Graduation speeches were delivered by my kids. Not all my kids graduated high school, but some did graduate later. I found peace in knowing that Hugo and I had taken them all farther than we got to go. We had given them Bible training as well and all of them grew up to be leaders, excelling in their professions. We had college graduates with Associates degrees, Bachelors degrees, and one Masters degree.

Lourene married Otto Falk, Jr. on July 3, 1970. Also in July Hugo reached the age of 65 and he retired.

In August of 1970 we visited my brother Charlie Corley who lived in El Campo, Texas. We always kept in touch with Charlie over the years and he visited us fairly regularly. Charlie had married a widow named Helen Wills who had three boys and Charlie raised those boys. Helen loved to decorate her home and she always used cloth tablecloths and decorative doilies. I was always nervous about the kids spilling stuff on her tablecloths or breaking her dishes, but she delighted in serving them with her best china. On one of our early visits she had intrigued LaVerne as she swept her lace tablecloth with a tiny brush and container after serving everyone cake and punch. LaVerne asked her about the tiny broom. She said, "I am crumbing," as she continued to whisk the crumbs from the tablecloth.

Helen brought culture to Charlie's life, but most of all, she brought him love. And, Charlie, even though he did not know who his father was, was able to be a good husband, father, and provider for Helen and her three boys. When we visited in August of 1970 Hugo, Alice, Sarah, and I stayed for two nights. All three of Charlie's stepsons were grown now. One of his granddaughters, Peggy Wills, was the same age as Alice. She came over to visit and the girls had a great time. We enjoyed our time with Charlie and Helen, just relaxing and talking. All too soon it was time to head home.

Shortly after we returned home Hugo was diagnosed with cancer. He began a long battle which would include surgery. We were praying for his healing and he was in church asking for prayer as well. 1971 was a busy year with all of Hugo's treatments. Alice graduated in May and when she left home in September the house seemed so very quiet; it bothered Hugo.

"That girl never says anything."

"What do you mean?" I retorted.

"Well, every night I sit here and I never hear Sarah saying anything in there. It's too quiet."

I laughed, "Hugo, there is no one for her to talk to. She wouldn't just be talking to herself!"

"I guess so," he conceded.

Sarah did soon make a close friend and chatter returned, but the first month after Alice left we all had to get used to a much quieter house.

Hugo went to Houston for chemotherapy treatments. He stayed with LaVerne and she drove him to the M.D. Anderson Cancer Center for the treatments. I went down there two different times and Sarah stayed with Virginia and James. It was difficult for me to miss work without putting my job in jeopardy. As a seamstress they cannot just get a worker to substitute for you. With furniture orders, quotas are important. If you are not there meeting your quota, you are not needed. I was not the fastest seamstress, but they could count on me. When I did it, it was well done. But I knew their policy, it was all about quotas. More than one person had lost their job because they couldn't keep up.

In the Spring of 1972 Hugo had surgery again and was hospitalized in Brenham. He was there on April 11 which was our 40th wedding anniversary. Some of our church friends brought a cake to the hospital and we celebrated "forty years together." We had done a lot of things together like farming with oxen, gardening, teaching babies to walk, working on cars, recovering our sofas to make them look like new, eating ice cream cones at 9:00 P.M. while we sat in the City Café parking lot waiting for Virginia to get off work, watching Tillman rise from the wheel chair, later accosting him at the railroad station when he disobeyed, riding around Lake Somerville just to watch the sunset – a lot of things.

We were still praying for Hugo's healing. The kids were routinely coming to visit at the hospital. The week of April 21 it seemed that death was imminent. Hugo asked Sister Williams to bring him communion which she did. He didn't want me to leave the hospital, even to go home to bathe and change clothes. It seemed like he knew that death was coming and he didn't want to be alone. LaVerne brought Alice to visit and when Alice got ready to leave, Hugo said to her, "If you are going to kiss me, Girlie, you better kiss me now."

The morning of April 28 he took my hand and he slowly said to me, "Nora Mae, you can go home now." I didn't leave, but I knew what he meant. He was ready to go; he died that day. He was 66 years old; I was 56.

It seemed so unfair. I was still working at Maddox, but Hugo had retired just 1 year and 9 months ago. Our lives had slowed down; our home was paid for. We had fewer responsibilities; only one kid, Sarah, was left at home. I didn't get it. I didn't want to be alone. I had prayed for God to heal him, to restore his life, but he wasn't healed. Hugo had to go on to a new home and I couldn't go with him. I reasoned, "God, it's me, Nora Mae. I'm the person who asked you to heal Alice of stuttering, to rescue Tillman from polio's grip, to heal Joyce of cancer, and a jillion other miracles that you granted. It's me, Nora Mae......." Yes, I reasoned, but that didn't change things.

A poet once had written "rich is the man who has friends." Hugo always had friends.

These verses are from Psalms 127 in the King James version of the <u>Bible</u>:

"Lo, children are an heritage of the LORD: and the fruit of the womb is his reward.

"As arrows are in the hand of a mighty man; so are children of the youth.

"Happy is the man who has his quiver full of them; they shall not be ashamed, but they shall speak with the enemies in the gate."

Hugo's quiver had been full. He had sent eleven arrows out into the world. He had definitely influenced the future and had enjoyed happiness. His children had surrounded him with love.

Here was another death for me to digest. He went to heaven's reward; I was left with emptiness. Death is as big a part of our journey as is our birth. Death is such a huge part of life you would think that everyone would prepare for it. We buried Hugo in the family plot with Henry.

It's silly, but I didn't want to be alone in the quiet house. Sarah became my chauffeur. Just two years earlier I was getting miffed at Hugo for always wanting to go somewhere.

Now it was ME! When I came home from work on Monday Sarah and I ate and then went to visit Aunt Pauline (a 15 minute drive), or Aunt Lucille and Uncle Pete (a 15 minute drive), or Brother and Sister Williams (a 10 minute drive). We rotated through the list.

On Tuesdays we went to church. On Thursdays we visited Virginia and James in Brenham (a 20 minute drive), or Lourene and Bubba in Bellville (a 30 minute drive), or Hugo and Dolores in Wellborn (a 30 minute drive). On Fridays we went to church. On the week-end some of the kids and their families would always come and visit us; every week-end for a full year and a half someone came faithfully. On Sundays we went to church in the morning and in the evening. Wednesday evening was the only evening that we stayed home. We cleaned house and mowed the yard on Wednesdays. Being with people and sharing their joys somehow nourished me. I was able to sing again, and gas wasn't that expensive.

Mama's health was going down during this time. Sarah and I would occasionally make the 30 minute drive to visit her on Sunday afternoons; she still lived with two of my half-sisters. She seemed more and more aloof. One Sunday afternoon when we visited there was a marked difference; Mama was definitely disoriented and she was having trouble walking to the chair. Trying to assist her, I discovered that her hip was badly bruised. When I asked my half-sisters about it they said that she had fallen in the bathtub and they hadn't told me. I tried to control my anger, but I said to them, "Mama may need more specialized care; we should check about a nursing home." Now one of my half-sisters got angry. Shortly, as Sarah and I were leaving, she emphatically said to me, "Nora Mae, don't come back."

The next time that Sarah and I went to visit they wouldn't answer the door. As we stood knocking on the front door in the cold and rain, my half-sister went out the back door, came around the house, and began hollering at us from the neighbor's driveway, "Get off my property!" We turned toward her as the rain began freezing and the ice pelted us in the face. She was not wearing a jacket and she stood barefooted in the freezing rain; she continued to yell angrily, "Get off my property!"

Sarah and I retreated to the car and left. It was such a strange occurrence. Bizarre. It bothered me. The next week Lourene and Bubba took their baby Cindy to visit Mama and they wouldn't let them in the house either. When another of my kids went to visit and they refused to let them see Mama too, Sarah said to me, "What if she's dead?"

"What? What do you mean?"

"Well, what if she died and they're just hiding her body so they can keep drawing her Social Security check? I just heard in the news about some people that did that. That could be why they won't let anyone see her."

"You're kidding."

"No. Some people really did that. Up north somewhere. It was just in the news. They could be hiding her body."

It was unbelievable, but possible.

Chapter 16

Teaching Grandma to Drive

---◇◇◇◇◇◇---

When Sarah had suggested to me that maybe Mama was dead and my half-sisters were hiding her body, I knew that was very unlikely, but the fact that it was possible was what haunted me. I couldn't get it out of my head and then there was also that badly bruised hip I'd seen. "You should at least have it checked out," kept popping into my mind.

I mentioned it to a friend and she confirmed, "You should check it out. They can't legally keep you from seeing your mother. You could get the deputy sheriff to accompany you."

So that's what I did. I asked the deputy sheriff to meet me at the property. I invited Hugo Jr. and his family to come also. It was a cold day when we went. The deputy approached the house first. When they didn't open the front door which had rags stuffed around it to help keep out the cold, we went around to the back door. They wouldn't open that door either. The deputy knocked again and again and finally they opened the wooden door, but not the screen door. I was standing behind the deputy.

My half-sister kept saying, "What are the charges? What are the charges, sir?"

"There are no charges; we just want to make sure that your mother is okay."

"She's fine. Everything is fine," she answered, but she didn't invite the deputy in.

"We want to see her."

"See her?"

"Yes. We came to see her."

They agreed to get Mama. We were standing out in the cold. They finally walked her to the door and they opened the screen door so we could see her. She appeared disoriented and her brown eyes displayed fear.

"Do you want to see your daughter?"

"Naw. Naw." Mama had earlier been diagnosed with Parkinson's and the deputy could barely hear her as she spoke, "Naw. Naw."

I wasn't sure what my half-sisters had told her, but I knew that she was confused and the terror in her eyes was heartbreaking. I wouldn't be allowed to hug her or to even talk to her that day, but I did see that she was alive.

After they closed the door, the deputy turned to me and said, "You may want to pursue this further. There is care available for her. It is disturbing to me that she could barely speak."

I didn't pursue it; that fear in her eyes got to me. It told me that she didn't really know me anymore and this visit had been traumatic for her.

That was the last time that I saw Mama alive. She lived eleven more years and I kept up with how she was doing through conversations with Charlie who lived in El Campo, my stepsisters who also lived miles away, and Hubert, my half-brother who lived about ten minutes from Mama. I asked Hubert to check on her regularly and I told him that I wouldn't be going to check on her anymore.

Ugh! More challenges in life! More hurts! More things to have to forgive! I made a decision to walk away. I had to consciously forgive my half-sister for barring me from the property. And, yes, I made peace in my heart with "Old Man" Brinkmann. God had made me feel that I had to forgive him too. When I let go of my hurt I began to see some good that he had done. He had cared for Mama and given her a home. He had worked hard to be sure we all ate. He had provided for his large family and taught them to be honest and lead productive lives.

It was like I had to forgive everyone who'd ever hurt me or used me or wronged me. For a while I thought God would just change my name to "Forgiveness." It's so hard to forgive, but so worth it; and all it is, is a decision on one's part to let go of or give up resentment against one who has wronged you. It is to pardon them or to overlook the offense, which is easier said than done and sometimes only possible with

God's help. At times you can only make yourself say, "I forgive them." God has to do the work in your heart. The incredible thing is that he does.

It's a mystery: only God's forgiveness can give us true life; but if we don't forgive others, God won't forgive us. If we don't forgive, it will kill the joy in our lives. Some doctors feel that "to not forgive" is a root cause of disease.[7] I believe that one's ability to forgive is a major contributor to their length of life.

In January of 1973 the United States combat role in Vietnam ended. Many people in our nation had to forgive war related offenses.

I was looking ahead and thinking about Sarah graduating in June. I knew that more than likely she would be leaving in September and I would be "grounded." Oh, I still rode to work with the carpool, but all my extracurricular outings would be over.

I still had a dream of driving a car; it was hidden somewhere, but it was still there. I decided that it was time to start working toward my dream. I asked Hugo Jr. if he would teach me to drive and he consented.

My first lesson was to drive on the sparsely traveled gravel road that went to the Somerville dump. We took my Impala. My grandchildren Cherie, Joel, and Tracie wanted to go along so we said that they could go.

"Come on! We're teaching Grandma to drive!" Joel announced.

The grandkids piled into the back seat and we took off. Hugo Jr. drove on the way out and I was to drive on the way back. He let me drive in the middle of the road. He wanted me to learn to start and stop, and to check the mirrors.

I took off slowly; it was kinda' fun. I checked the mirrors. The kids were giggling in the back seat. I was going about 15 miles per hour.

"You need to get a feel for the brakes," Hugo Jr. said. "Do you see that shadow up ahead?"

"Yes."

"When you get to the shadow start stopping. See how long it takes you to stop."

"Okay!"

When we reached the shadow, I was thinking, "It won't take me long to stop." I hit the brake and the car gave a powerful jerk. Everyone flew forward as we skidded a bit on the gravel (this car did not have seat belts). In the silence I heard sniffling. Tracie who had been sitting in the middle in the back was crying. Her lip had busted as she flew into the back of the seat. It was bleeding.

"Gosh, Grandma!"

Rats! Wouldn't you know it! Anything could happen with me driving.

"Put the car in park," Hugo Jr. offered. "When you brake you have to hit the brake slowly."

"Now you tell me." This was very different than braking a Model T. "I thought you said to see how long it would take me to stop."

"I didn't know you were gonna' stomp it. You have to tap it slowly; don't worry, you'll get the feel of it."

I put it in park. We checked Tracie's bleeding mouth; only her lip was cut. When they saw that she was okay, the kids started laughing. Before long, I was laughing too. We all laughed. Joel never let me live that down. Tracie was okay, but now I was more nervous.

"Let's try it again," Hugo Jr. said and I took off.

When I got ready to try the brake the next time he said, "Make sure your hands are on Tracie in the back seat. We don't want her flying again!"

I did much better on the second try and by the time we finished the lesson, my braking was smooth.

That was good for a first lesson, but I had a long way to go. I had been the only car on the road and I had taken the middle of the road. But I was eager to drive again.

"I can drive! I can drive!" I savored it.

Hugo Jr. and his family came again the next week-end and we went out again. His idea was for me to learn to drive across a bridge. We took the road out of Somerville that went to Chris Balke's place. There were three old wooden bridges on this road and they were narrow.

"Come on! We're teaching Grandma to drive!" Joel informed the other grandkids and they piled in. They didn't want to miss it.

Once more, Hugo Jr. drove on the way out. "As you cross the bridge keep your eye on the side window – make sure you see the edge of the bridge and keep the steering straight." He demonstrated.

Now it was my turn to drive. As we approached the first bridge I slowed way down. We crossed it, inch by inch.

"Try going a little faster on the next one."

"It was kinda' scary; sitting in the middle of the bridge. It's so far down," Joel offered.

"I kept it straight even if it was slow," I defended my performance.

On the second bridge I went a bit faster, keeping it straight all the way. "You did it!" the grandkids cheered.

On the third one I barely slowed down. "I'm a real driver," I thought.

When we got home the kids were talking about going over the bridges. Joyce and her family had come in while we were out and she was listening intently, "What bridges are you talking about?"

"You know those old ones on the way to Mr. Balke's place." Mr. Balke was her father-in-law.

"Those old bridges! You're kidding me. I don't ever drive over those narrow bridges myself, if I can help it." Joyce giggled.

Really? I had done it! Successfully.

When the transmission suddenly went out on my Impala, my son-in-law Bubba Falk sold me his white Dodge Coronet for $500. Sarah and I were still traveling. After she graduated in June I started some serious practice driving. I drove at Lake Somerville and we went to Caldwell so I could get a book to study for my written test.

Alice got married to Bill Schiel that June. She was the only one of my kids that planned their wedding with me. We went to see Ruth Strickland and selected the cake from her book. Ruth was "tops" for cakes in Somerville and the surrounding area. Her little singly-made roses would be very expensive in our day of mass production; she made them individually. We also ordered Ruth's famous white sherbet punch that was created with vanilla mellorine (do you even know what that is), pineapple sherbet, pineapple juice, and ginger ale – oh, so many calories, but so appropriate for a grand celebration! Ruth also took care of our flower order and she would provide the crystal cake plates and punch cups for the reception. I made the pillow for the ring bearer to carry and helped with sewing dresses and neckties. The wedding was beautiful and the whole family helped with the clean-up.

My dream of driving really began to come alive now. By the time Sarah left for Midwest Bible Institute that fall, I was a fairly confident driver.

Lourene had played piano at the Apostolic Faith Church we attended, Hugo Jr's wife Dolores had played, and Alice had played from the time she was in sixth grade until she left home. Her classmate Betsy Neinast was pianist at the Lutheran Church and her classmate George Pazdral was pianist at the Presbyterian Church. Three church pianists were in the same class at school. When Alice left home Sarah began to play piano at church and she played for two years. When Sarah left home we had no pianist; but a church has to have music, right? I mean, our spirits soar with music! I was determined that I would learn to play the piano, but there was no longer a piano teacher in Somerville.

When Hugo had died I had purchased a piano for the church with memorial funds and it needed to be praising! I purchased some "teach yourself to play" materials and I started working at it. The house didn't seem so empty with me busy studying and practicing. I stayed home evenings and practiced on the piano. Finally I was good enough to accompany singing. It was a happy day when I was able to bang out a few songs with the singers at church!

Now that I had conquered a few songs I was ready to roll again. Sitting at the piano in the evening no longer totally consumed me; I wanted to "go!" I focused on the driver's license: "I can do this!" In 1974 I got my license. It felt so good to have climbed that mountain and reached one of my dreams! I was as excited about driving as any teen-ager! Finally, I could participate in driving in the carpool to work; I could go visit whenever I wanted; I could drive to church; I could drive my own trash to the dump.

Learning to drive and learning to play the piano were two goals that I reached almost simultaneously. I continued to play the piano at church for about 17 years. I never really mastered it and when guest pianists visited I gladly deferred to them, but no one ever worshipped from the piano more than I; I gave it my all. It's a funny thing but God likes to work through our weakness. It seems that's where He gets the most glory. Somerville had a television channel for a while and we had a TV crew that recorded and broadcast our church services. The most unlikely thing occurred: I was in the broadcast, playing the piano. God definitely uses the foolish things to confound the wise and I can truthfully say that I played piano on television! (There are many good pianists that can't say that.)

Our journey on earth contains many surprises! My piano playing was just one of those. Richard Bach said, "Here is a test to find whether your mission on Earth is finished: If you are alive, it isn't." In 1974 I turned 58 years old; I was still not 2/3 of the way through my journey. Much of my mission was ahead of me.

On September 18, 1975 Charlie died. What a lot of memories flooded me. At his funeral they acknowledged that he was raised by his mother and stepfather. That old unanswered question, "who is Charlie's father", popped into my head. His name was Charlie Corley so everyone, outside of family, assumed that we had the same father.

I remembered that day long ago when Charlie had worn the new overalls and eagerly waited to meet his father. Of course, no one had ever come. I closed my eyes. Over the years some family members guessed who they thought Charlie's father was. Mama never confirmed any of the guesses and she never told Charlie or me who his father was; to us it remained an unanswered mystery. It didn't really matter. Charlie died at age 56 having been a good son, a good brother, a good husband, and a good father.

Ken and Marian Feick moved into the house next door to me in 1976. The Eldridge boys brought the Feick girls over to meet me. Donna was twelve; Karen was seven; Cathy, five. The girls were friendly and full of energy.

The next day when I arrived home from work, the girls came over. I was dog-tired, but seeing those three happy faces seemed to energize me. My routine was to check my garden before I prepared my evening meal. I loved fresh vegetables and many times my evening meal would be fresh vegetables. This day I visited with the chatty girls who stayed about an hour and then went home.

They rushed over again the next day as I pulled into the driveway so I invited them to accompany me to the garden. Surprisingly, they seemed to like the garden and were excited when I sent some vegetables home with them.

They ran over again the third evening and stayed a couple of hours.

"Won't your mother be needing you at home to set the table and help her get supper ready?"

"Oh, no! Mom works at the liquor store from three to nine at night. She's not home right now."

"Well, what about your daddy?"

"He does maintenance at the school. Dad will be home soon."

A pattern developed: the girls would visit me or the Barton sisters who lived across the street, in the early evenings until their dad got home which was 7:00 to 7:30 PM. They would bring their homework and we would work in the garden and then do homework. I purchased a quilt frame which Hugo Jr. helped me hang and I let the girls watch me do the quilting stitches; I played piano for them; they helped me feed the chickens.

"You have so much stuff to do," they noted. "We like it here!"

Their mother eventually opened a florist shop in town so her work hours changed, but our friendship continued. (Even after they grew up and got married they returned to visit, to show me their babies or just to keep in touch.) It was too much for me to try to teach all three girls to quilt at once, so I invited them to lunch individually on Saturday and let them do the quilt stitches. I loved sharing the craft and they liked trying the stitches.

Their dad hated cats so their family choice of pet was the dog; they had several. Donna really wanted a cat and when she found a stray kitty she hid it in her bedroom for two weeks before her parents found it.

"That cat has to go."

The girls ran over and begged me to let their kitty stay at my house.

"We will take care of it. It will be no bother for you. We will buy the food. We just need a place for it to stay. Please! Please!"

I thought, "Yeah, right. No trouble. No cat hair. No kitty litter box. No future kittens."

They were surprised and disappointed when I gave them an emphatic, "No."

Marian did convince Ken to let them keep the kitten.

"It's already been here two weeks and it's been no trouble; we should let them keep it."

Chapter 17

Redirection in Pink

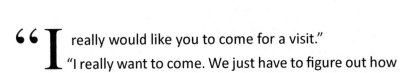

"I really would like you to come for a visit."

"I really want to come. We just have to figure out how I can get home."

In the late seventies Sarah was part of a mission team residing in Reynosa, Mexico caring for orphaned or abandoned children. When Sarah first arrived at the orphanage they had given her a room in the overseer's house. A few weeks later she was assigned a room in the girl's dorm. She had written about hiding under the covers at night because she could hear mice scurrying around in her room. The Mexican lady residing there with the children just thought that mice were a part of life. Sarah purchased a trap and caught one immediately so she set the trap again; she caught another…and another…and another. She eventually caught more than forty mice in her room! She had conquered the rodents and things were better now. She had come home for a visit and wanted me to go back with her for a few days so I could meet the children who had stolen her heart.

"There's an airport in McAllen. You could ride down with me and then catch a plane back to Houston."

"I really do want to go. I've never flown before so that would be great. Hopefully I wouldn't get sick or anything."

"I'm sure you wouldn't. People fly every day."

"Let's do it."

We planned all the details including who would drive me to the McAllen Airport and who would drive me from Houston Intercontinental to my home in Somerville. It was doable. I rode down with Sarah and was excited to meet the children: Charita, Rosa, Paco, Wency, Carlos, Patricia, Sabino; I can't remember them all.

I was relieved to not have any encounters with mice! Sarah demanded that the children wear their shoes. Some churches had held shoe drives to help them control the worm issues that were a part of life in Reynosa. If the kids wore shoes they wouldn't be as likely to get tapeworms which can enter the body through the feet. Shoes were an easy solution to a serious problem. The kids would always try to sneak out barefooted anyway.

I enjoyed keeping up with the orphanage routines and also did fine on the flight home – modern me!

Sarah spent two years at the orphanage.

Early in 1980 I began to struggle at work. It was getting harder and harder for me to keep up with my daily quota of cushions sewn; either I was moving slower or my sight was weakening. I tried pushing myself more, leaving late for break; but nothing helped, even my singing rhythms were not enough. I was 64 years old and wanted to wait until age 65 to draw my Social Security pension so I would have the highest amount of money possible for me. I was heartbroken in July when I received a pink slip – July 15, 1980 would be my last day. I was eight months short of my 65th birthday. That pink slip meant that I would have to find another job and more than likely my last year's pay would lower the average for the amount of Social Security pension that I could receive when I reached 65. I could keep my medical insurance, but I needed to get a job right away in order to keep my payments current.

I would have to see what God would provide for me. I packed up my huge scissors and said good-bye to my friends at work; I had been sewing there for twenty years. I would miss my carpool friends the most – Nylene Harris, Louise Glass, Harold Quebe, and Mr. and Mrs. Milton Bosse. Our conversations on the fifteen mile trip to and from work were some of the most interesting times of my day. I would be closing that door and opening a new one; to what, I had no idea. I inquired around Somerville to see what jobs were available and was grateful when Strickland's Variety hired me as cashier, stocker, and "do it all" person. Somerville is a small town so jobs opportunities were limited. Again, I was very grateful to have a job!

Since the landscape of my journey was changing I anticipated whatever was ahead. I had another dream tucked away in my heart and I wanted to pursue it: I still wanted a high school diploma. I was sure that I could do the necessary work. From Dorothy's first day of school in 1939 to Sarah's last day in 1973 was a period of 34 years; that, plus my seven school years was a total of 41 years that I had done homework! I was sure that I at least knew as much as my kids did. I remember the girls asking me,

"Mama, my spelling test is tomorrow. Would you please call the words out to me?" or "Mama, my science test is tomorrow; would you help me with the review?"

I would lay the word list or the review packet on the counter and call out the questions while I was cooking supper. I was still doing homework with the Feick girls. I had reviewed Texas History, US History, World History, the Sciences, Spanish, Geography – you name it, I had reviewed it, many times. And what about math? I had kept up with the basics and numbers were still like music to me.

When I heard that a class for obtaining a GED was being offered in the Somerville area I was thrilled and signed up as quickly as I could. Lillian Brinkman was teaching those evening classes. She and I always rode together on the 4 mile trip from Somerville to the Lyons Community Center. I was delighted to complete all the required coursework and pass the tests for my diploma in February of 1981. I was finished so Lillian drove to the next class alone. She had a car wreck and was killed while en route. The community had lost a treasure.

Obtaining a GED diploma seems a small accomplishment to many, but to me, it felt like I had climbed Mt. Kilimanjaro (the highest free standing mountain in the world).

The whole family was excited for me and planned a party for my 65th birthday which was on March 13th. The party would be on March 14th. Hugo Jr's wife Dolores made me a cake that was shaped like an open book. One side was decorated to show my driver's license obtained, the other depicted my GED diploma. Two dreams that seemed to elude me had been obtained. My heart sang!

I continued to work at Strickland's Variety where I worked with Hattie Sears who had been working there for years. Hattie was about my age, had short gray hair, glasses, a broad smile, and a hearty laugh. She had always befriended my kids who had stopped in to buy candy. We got along really well; both of us were responsible workers so the job was enjoyable. One Friday we had gotten our checks and on lunch break had gone to the bank and cashed them. We put our purses in the usual spot under the counter below the cash register.

"Nora Mae, I am going to the back of the store to check the stuff that needs to be put on the shelves. I shouldn't be long."

"Okay."

Shortly, two tall black men that I did not recognize entered the store; they proceeded to stomp around, looking at the merchandise. Presently, one of them approached the counter, "I can't find the washrags."

"You were almost to them; they are on that last row of shelves," I pointed.

""I looked over that way and didn't see them. Would you please show me where they are?"

"Sure."

I walked with him to the washrags. He picked some up, looking at them slowly and carefully.

"What is the price of the blue ones?"

"The price is there on the package. There are five in the package."

"Are the striped ones the same price? Do you have any singly priced ones for sale?"

He asked other similar questions about all of the washrags as he picked them up and surveyed each bundle.

After a few minutes he put everything down and said, "I don't see exactly what I had in mind. Maybe next time."

He walked to the front of the store and both men stomped out. Strange.

I straightened the washcloths on the shelf before I returned to the front of the store. When I went around the counter I could immediately see that both of our purses had been opened. I snatched up my purse; my wallet was gone; that meant that all of my paycheck was gone. The one man had distracted me with the washrags while the other had stolen our money. He had probably spotted the items on that last row on his first walk around the store. I couldn't believe it, but we had, flat out, been robbed!

I rushed to the front door and looked out, but the men were nowhere to be seen; the sidewalk was empty. I ran to get Hattie; she confirmed that her wallet was gone too. I called the deputy sheriff who came to investigate, but none of our stuff was ever found. Nothing else in the store was taken. I had to get a new driver's license, insurance cards, etc. It was a set back to my budget, but I pinched and made it.

My general trust in mankind took a hit. My feelings of being safe in a small town evaporated. I began to lock my doors faithfully and I rented a safe deposit box at the bank for my important papers. I am still shocked that people will steal from old folks. They will steal from nice people; we have to be diligent and "as wise as serpents."

My granddaughter Tracie was having a twirling competition in Houston. Her parents were working so I agreed to accompany Shirley (Eldridge) Ladewig who was driving the girls down. The kids had a splendid time and I loved sitting in the bleachers for hours (oops – no stretching the truth), I loved watching their performance and feeling their excitement! As we traveled home the hood flew up on a truck in the oncoming lane. The driver crossed into our lane and we crashed. We were wearing our seat belts, but were banged up and received minor injuries; I had cuts on my knee and my chin. The chin bled a lot. When the ambulance workers secured me on the stretcher for the transport to Tomball Hospital there was so much blood all around my neck that Tracie began to cry hysterically.

"Granny! Granny! Your head's cut off! Your head's cut off!"

I tried to sit up. "Explain to her that I'm okay!" I demanded. The EMT crew kept carrying me toward the ambulance.

"Calm down, Ma'am."

Shirley comforted Tracie. We all survived the ordeal.

Chapter 18

Babysitting

In January of 1982 we had a severe cold spell. There was snow and sleet lingering on the ground and I was afraid to drive on the ice so decided to walk to work. It was icy, but I made it. The temperature remained freezing or just above freezing all day; the walk home that afternoon was challenging. It was so cold that it was hard to breathe as I walked. That night my chest began to hurt tremendously. I argued with myself,

"You could be having a heart attack!"

"Calm down, Nora Mae. More than likely it's really bad heartburn."

"You should call someone."

"Are you kidding? They would probably have a wreck getting over here; the roads are so bad."

"Call the ambulance."

"No. The roads are too bad."

"You should at least call Son."

"No. It's sleeting again. If I call him, he'll probably risk his life rushing over here to find me with indigestion."

"Then just go to bed."

"Okay."

I went to bed. I had such a painful night that it scared me, so early the next morning I called Sister Williams and asked her to pray for me and I called Bo Norris' wife Linda and asked her to drive me to Brenham to St. Jude's Hospital. She did; it was cold, but the road was not as bad as I had feared. When we checked in at the hospital, someone there called my daughter Virginia who was working at Sweetbriar Nursing Center not far away.

"Your mother's had a heart attack. You need to come right over."

Virginia came right over. The next day I experienced congestive heart failure and the tremendous fluid buildup in and around my heart led the doctor to report to my kids, who had converged upon the place,

"If she survives this night, she has a chance to make it."

It seemed like a long night, but I made it through. The prayers of my friends and family had moved God's hand to restore me. I was released from the hospital.

Nellene had come from Arkansas where she now lived; she stayed a few days to help me. My home health nurse was Geneva Gonzales who had been Alice's classmate in school. Geneva checked my vitals and she told Nell and Sarah,

"Don't be surprised if he wants to put her back in the hospital tomorrow."

That statement caused fear to rise in my heart. Sarah reminded me, "Do not be afraid. The devil brings fear, but he is a liar." Her little reminder brought my faith level up a notch.

When Nell and I went for my check-up the next day the doctor did not suggest putting me back in the hospital. He, instead, scheduled me a trip to Houston for specialists to do a camera test in my heart. The kids took turns staying with me the next two weeks. They had me sleeping on the couch or sitting in the chair so they could keep an eye on me; they wanted to make sure I was okay. At the end of the second week when Sarah came to stay she had no idea that I had been sleeping on the couch. She offered to sleep on the couch to be nearer my bedroom; I happily returned to my bed.

I made the trip to Houston and the test result was amazing! They said that they couldn't tell that I'd ever had a heart attack. There was no visible damage to my heart – none, zero, zilch! God had powerfully touched me. That was the first time I traveled to the brink of death (other than eleven childbirths) and walked away; I was completely restored and at age 65, was very thankful.

On April 3, 1982 Sarah got married. She had been gone from home for 8 ½ years, but it was still my baby getting married. She married Neftali Muñoz who was from El Salvador. I was worried about her embracing a different culture, but she had been involved with Spanish speaking cultures (Mexican, El Salvadoran, Hispanic, Guatemalan) ever since she had gone to language school in the fall of 1977 and she had not the slightest concern. In time she won me over.

From 1981 to 1985 I did week-end babysitting for three of my grandkids. The grandkid list was always growing. Cindy was born in 1971, Hope in 1973, Suzanne in 1974, Alyssa in 1975, Josh and Billy in 1977, Byron in 1982, Julie in 1984, and Lee in 1985. Between 1981 and 1985 I was babysitting Virginia's three: Tracie, Hope, and Josh on the week-ends that their parents were working. The kids would arrive on Friday evening and stay until Sunday evening. We had so many fun times together. The first of my grandkids all called me "Grandma." Virginia taught her kids to call me "Granny" and all grandchildren born after Tracie did the same.

A visit to Granny's has to have something special so I would always have bananas, Rice Krispie treats, or banana pudding. When it was cold I made hot chocolate for them; Josh would try to sneak into my pantry, lick his finger, and put it in the chocolate powder mix. I told him not to, but he did it anyway. Once I swatted him with the fly swatter and it frightened him, but not enough to make him stop doing it. Those kids would try to climb into my attic, they did flips on the bed, and jumped on my treasured trunk. The Eldridge boys from down the road climbed on my roof and tried to convince my grandkids to follow.

"Stay off the roof!"

Where did they get so much energy? It took a lot of spunk to keep up with them.

The thing that I enjoyed the most about having the grandkids come and stay with me was that I got to take them with me to church. It seemed that we were always running late. How I ever efficiently managed eleven children, I wondered. Now I was out of breath just keeping up with three. (Actually the most I ever had living at home at one time was seven kids.)

"Everyone in the car. We gotta' go!"

It seemed that we always left in a hurry. The Apostolic Faith Church was basically three small town blocks from my house so I was never driving very fast. We could have walked, but then I would have been dealing with kids wandering off. At least the car kept us altogether while we were en route. One Sunday as we drove to church I went another way. I drove two blocks and as I slowly made a left turn the front passenger door opened and Tracie rolled into the street. Her door wasn't even shut! I braked and reached for her as she struggled to get up.

"Oh, my! Hurry up and get in. We're going to be late!" I called. My brain gave me another message: "Nora Mae, stop and check on the kid!"

I put it in park and gave her a spit bath and a band-aid. She was wearing the puffy purple dress she had worn in the Brenham Maifest Parade. I was relieved that she and her beautiful dress were fine.

"Let's go!"

To help keep the grandkids quiet in church I bribed them with Luden's cough drops. Funny, I never did that for my kids; they just had to button their lips, but these were grandkids, you know.

One Saturday I butchered a chicken for them. (You're never too young to learn.) I don't think they will ever forget that chicken flopping around without its head. I had kept a few chickens over the years, but needed to get rid of them because I was taking a new job as a caretaker and I would not be home to feed them daily. I was going to work for Mr. and Mrs. August Peters. I would be driving a few miles away and staying to take care of them during the week. I could still be home on week-ends to enjoy the grandkids and any of the rest of my family who would come to visit.

Virginia's kids would try to sneak to the Circle K convenience store that was just around the corner from my house. Josh would stand look-out and the two girls, who were older, would sneak to the store and run back. They thought that I never saw them. At the time Tracie was thirteen years old and I could see the Circle K from a bedroom window so I didn't let on that I knew......at least I think I knew every time that they went.

On February 11, 1984 Mama died. Of course, I had lost her much earlier. My family did participate in the funeral to celebrate her life and honor her memory. Eight days later, on February 19, 1984 my grandson Jimmie Lynn Balke died.

Jimmie who was Joyce and Billy's son was only 28 years old and he left behind his wife Nancy and their daughter Lisa. This was a lot for my heart to process – not only my grief, but my pain for my daughter Joyce.

I was thriving by being involved helping people – at church, I was teaching and providing rides for folks; at work – I was helping the Peters; on week-ends – my 3 grandkids came regularly every other week-end and the rest of the family visited often. Focusing on helping other people made it easier for me to walk through my grief. After Mr. Peters died, other arrangements were made for Mrs. Peters and I became the caretaker for Mrs. Hope Moore.

One day my telephone rang and as I answered I was surprised to hear the voice of one of my half-sisters. This was my half-sister who had ordered me off her property and refused to let me see my mother. She was talking rather quickly and my brain was in shock so I had to ask her to repeat what she had said.

"Nora Mae, it's me. My sister and I need to go to the specialist in Brenham. Would you be able to give us a ride? We will pay for your gas. We need to go on Thursday."

I was silent for a moment. My brain was clicking. You want me to drive 18 miles to Caldwell to get you, then drive thirty or so miles to Brenham, then drive thirty or so miles back to your place, and then 18 miles back home. That's roughly 96 miles! I couldn't believe that she was asking me for anything after she had treated me so badly. She had been WRONG!

Other thoughts took her side: they had no way to get to Brenham and they needed the medical help. But there was no, "I'm sorry I mistreated you," it was just a request......I had forgiven them, hadn't I?

I could hardly do it, but I made myself say it,

"I can do it on Thursday. What time do you have to be there?" Thus I became their transportation for several years. Neither of them had ever married so they had no children to help them. I had to remind myself over and over again that I had forgiven them, but eventually a softness came and my heart believed it too. I was determined to not be an empty shell, to let life flow through me.

The 1980's brought an oil boom to Burleson County, Texas. Leases had been signed in the seventies and the 1980's brought money to many landowners. The Hein properties along highway 36 were a part of the Austin Chalk Geological Formation which housed the oil that was now being pumped. I was hopeful!

Chapter 19

Snafu

This chapter reveals what I consider my greatest blunders, my biggest regret. I really want to leave this chapter out, because it shows weakness. A key thing I try to remember is that I faced my failures and moved on. You may have similar experiences in your life and I hope that you too can admit your debacles and let your spirit overrule your human frailty. Life is about ups and downs so here goes-

In the 1970's leases were signed and in the 1980's the production of oil in Burleson County, Texas brought monetary blessings to many.

The Hein family is a large, but closely knit family. The Hein Family Reunion for the descendants of Johann (John) Hein, who lived from 1840 to 1899 and was Hugo's grandfather, started in 1963 and continues to meet every year in June. (In 2015 they held the 53rd reunion.) Neither Hugo nor I ever missed one of the reunions during our lifetime. After Hugo's death I remained close to his family so I knew that oil was produced on the Hein properties which had been part of a Spanish land grant to Frank Dungen and some family members were well compensated. There were no "Jed Clampets" and no one got filthy rich, but they did receive royalties. I couldn't understand why I never received anything. I knew that the property Hugo's mom had given us and we gave back to her to repay our loan in 1938 was a part of the leased pool and I was positive that we had kept at least part of our mineral rights.

I went to the courthouse and was surprised that there was no record of our transactions. It was like the deeds were never filed, but we had moved eight times since then and I couldn't find them. Hugo had been dead since 1972 therefore I could not ask him about the deeds. I knew that I should have received royalties but couldn't prove it. I was so sure that we had kept some of the mineral rights that I wondered if someone had cheated us, but was advised that we must have never filed our deed so it was of no effect. In common terms, it was like my ship came in, but sailed right past me. The money went to someone else and I had to let it go. (Let it go, Nora Mae.)

What could have happened to our deed? Many years were to pass before I found the answer.

Important lesson learned – when you buy or sell property make sure your deed is filed at the courthouse. Just because a lawyer handles your transaction that does not mean that he automatically files your deed.

It wasn't like I had to have that money to survive. I could get along on my social security. I was confident that God would supply my need if any extra expenses came up. Once I had been down to my last 75 cents. I still had bills to pay and needed groceries. I had felt compelled to put the 75 cents in the offering at church instead of buying needed milk or flour. I gave the money to the kids to put in the Sunday School offering. When we got home from church, someone had left 2 bags of groceries on the porch! I was amazed! I had been repaid many times over from an unexpected and unknown source. I never found out who had left the groceries. That miracle had taught me to not worry about finances; as long as I was staying within my budget, I knew that any unexpected expenses would be provided for or a door would open for me to earn the cash I needed.

During the 1980's our church seemed to grow smaller and smaller. I was doing more and more because there was no one else to help out. After Sister Williams' husband Laney died at age 80 in January of 1985, I began to mow the church lawn. Since she had never learned to drive I began driving to Lyons to give her a ride to Somerville to church. We now had regular services on Sunday morning, Sunday evening, and on Thursday evening. I picked up Tillie Schoppe and Sister Williams for each service.

I don't know if other churches in Somerville had a decline in attendance in the eighties or not, but I do know that participation in the community ministerial alliance dwindled some. I began to attend the meetings because I was Sister Williams' ride and lay people were welcomed. I became treasurer for the group whose main activities were <u>Bible</u> study, a community-wide Thanksgiving service in November, and a community-wide sunrise service on Easter morning. It was a sharing time for all Christians regardless of church affiliation. I enjoyed being treasurer; other folks struggled with numbers, trying to get everything to come out right; for me the numbers seemed to line right up. The group was more than happy for me to be treasurer.

Being a part of the Somerville/Lyons Ministerial Alliance allowed me to make new friends. I also worked a bit at Ron's Lawnmower Shop and there I met a man name Don who made me laugh a lot. He asked me out on a date and I accepted. The romantic interest made me feel young; I was more than just a grandma! We both thought it was fascinating that my phone number was 596-1926 and his was 596-2027. I was shopping for another car and Don gave me advice. I purchased a yellow Plymouth that he located for me. Don and I hit it off and after a courtship we had fun planning our wedding. Blue would be the main color. We got married on April 17, 1988 and then traveled to Michigan so I could meet his family.

My girls had cautioned me before the wedding, "Mama, you know you can't stand cigarette smoking."

But even old folks in love must be blind. I ignored their advice. Don did smoke, but always outside and never with me. After a great first year things went sour. We had huge differences of opinion in a few areas and those surfaced. He had never drank alcohol around me during our courtship and never during our first year of marriage, but all of a sudden he wanted to drink a beer whenever he felt like it. He also smoked in my car which made me angry. Later he smoked in the house and that made me feel ill. He had evidently enjoyed drinking and smoking all his life and had only abstained because he knew I was against that life style.

I was not willing to live with alcohol in the house because of my past experiences. I did not want alcohol in my home and definitely was not willing to subject myself to second-hand smoke. I felt betrayed and experienced tears, worry, and anger. There were no young children involved so, after counseling, I shamefully moved back to my house in town to contemplate what to do. One evening the phone rang. It was Don. He had called to tell me that he had filed for a divorce. He didn't want me to be "taken off guard" when they served me the divorce papers. Our marriage ended in November of 1989. We remained friends and talked of possibly trying again, but he died nine months after our divorce.

The wedding had been a huge mistake. All the lovely wedding pictures we had made were now a farce. Living alone didn't look so bad to me anymore. This anonymous quote can help bring clarity to handling ones blunders,

"Our greatest glory is not in never failing, but in rising every time we fall."

Thankfully, this chapter is finished – let's move on -

Chapter 20

Getting Older, Doing More

Three things happened around 1990 that were symbols to me of new life, freshness. First, Reverend Robert Tompkins and his wife Shirley started driving from Hempstead to attend our church and it was like the church started breathing again. Our attendance began to go up. Second, my daughter LaVerne retired and moved back to Burleson County after being gone from the area forty-one years. I was excited to have her living only 15 minutes away. She checked on me often. I think the animals of Burleson County were the most happy to see her; that girl rescued more critters than I could keep up with. The veterinarian in Caldwell was probably one of the first people she became acquainted with. She brought hope to people and animals alike because a sense of caring radiated from her. The birth of my grandson Benjamin Schiel in September was the third event symbolizing new beginnings. He is my youngest grandchild. I was now 74 years old.

In 1991 Robert and Shirley Tompkins moved to Somerville and became our pastors. Sister Williams was older than me and she realized her need to step down. I had known Brother Robert for many years having met him at youth rallies before 1960. Since I had known him from his youth, he was always "Brother Robert" to me, not Brother Tompkins. As new people began to come to church and take responsibility I was able to step down from teaching Sunday School. Brother Robert was a good guitarist and people liked to hear him sing. I played piano by note and couldn't play songs without written music so I was no longer needed as a pianist, but I still loved to sing and I was continually giving people rides to church. We changed the name of the church from Apostolic Faith Church to Community Chapel.

Rev. Modschiedler who had been pastoring in Michigan passed away and his wife returned to live in the home they had in Somerville (the one we had rented for about seven years). I worked for her off and on helping her with whatever she needed help with.

There was a man who came to church that was a big fella'. He attended services regularly for quite a while. He gave testimony that he had been abusive to his family in the past, but was now a changed man. He was still a rough looking character who wore dark glasses to church and was very outspoken. When he first came he only interrupted the sermon with things like "Amen" or "Preach it, brother." But the longer he was there the more comfortable he became.

He declared himself a minister and would interrupt services with remarks. One Sunday he stood up and made a comment to challenge one of the points in the sermon. I could not believe the audacity of this guy! He made another comment.

I thought, "Nora Mae, control yourself."

I am usually a nice, soft-spoken woman, but this was rubbing me the wrong way. The man continued to talk as he walked to the front of the church and stood beside Brother Robert. This was Brother Robert's first pastorate; he had limited experience to go on. I sensed that the man was trying to influence the congregation more than clarify a point.

I kept telling myself, "Nora Mae, control yourself."

Then I recanted, "No, go for it!"

I stood up, all of my five feet and one inch, looked the big guy straight in the eye, and said in a loud, stern voice, "Mister, you are out of line! You will not talk to my pastor that way. Set yourself down!" I glared at him.

Immediately there was silence in the church. The guy was shocked. Well, the whole church was shocked. Even I was shocked; I was a nice old woman. Did I really just do that?

The man turned and walked from the platform, straight out the back door of the church without another word. (He never came back. Hallelujah!) I sat down and Brother Robert continued his sermon as if nothing out of the ordinary had occurred. He laughed about it many times later, but he knew that, in that moment, I had been his backbone.

Ever since my heart attack in 1982 I viewed life as a gift. I made plans to die and purchased a burial policy, but I kept focusing on living. I never had a lot of money to give so I gave my time. I began to visit people in the Leisure Lodge nursing home in Caldwell. At first I visited my friends, but soon I became a volunteer who visited most of the people who lived there. Surprisingly, many of them were younger than me. When St. Joseph took over the facility I drove to the new location.

I had always been thankful to people who passed along gently used clothes for my kids. Mrs. Grace Laferney who lived in Somerville and had four daughters, once passed along some dresses to Alice. Sarah was a bit taller and couldn't use any of those, but her cousin Gayle Hein who was tall sent some for her. Interesting, of my eight girls three were short (around 5 feet I ¾ inches), three were medium (around 5 feet 4 ½ inches), and two were tall and slender (around 5 feet 6 ¼ inches).

Anyway, I started pondering a resale shop for the community where gently used items could be resold at low prices. I had visited such a shop in Tomball, Texas with my daughter Alice a few times. I knew that one of those would be helpful for our community, but how could we get it started? We could plan to give some items away if there was a great need or if a pastor requested it for someone, but selling things at low prices would provide money to pay to rent a decent building to house the ministry. Money from sales could also provide cash to help people with other needs.

I wanted to give back to this wonderful community of people who had welcomed me and my family and over the years had celebrated with us and cried with us. Always remember that when you help those who are struggling it helps everyone; do not make them dependent on you, just give them a boost. How many times had a small boost fed the inner hope which kept me going? I can't tell you how many times.

I was not the only one with such an idea. We discussed the resale shop idea at the Ministerial Alliance meetings. Many people didn't think that folks needed help. Others thought that we might get stuck with a bunch of old clothes that no one would want and just waste our time. Some people thought that it was a good idea, but couldn't commit to help. A handful of us were eager to start. I prayed about it a lot. After discussing the idea at several meetings a small group of us felt that we needed to do it.

"We can't just keep talking about it. We must take action."

So we took the name Somerville Community Action Team. Our acronym was SCAT. The year was 1994. After we donated our own clothing, a few pastors announced to their congregations that we were collecting clothes and the contributions began. Reverend Virgil Pecht, Shirley Tompkins, Mattie Mae Sweeney, myself, and a few others collected the clothes. We sorted them and I took items that needed washing and mending home with me. Nothing would be sold unless all the buttons were on and the seams trustworthy. I became the treasurer for our group, handling the bank deposits and paying the expenses.

The main problem we faced was for a place to house all the items. Brother Pecht allowed us to use rooms at the Lutheran Church for a short while. We rented a few different houses to set up everything for our sale days. Initially we, the volunteers, contributed the money to pay the rent ourselves. Gradually we were able to pay it from SCAT funds, but we had no permanent building to house the ministry. Moving everything for sale day was a huge undertaking. We finally settled into an old house by the elementary school until we outgrew it.

We did help a lot of people and slowly we were proving that the Somerville community could maintain such a ministry. Funds from sales helped us stock a food pantry. My friends at church were astonished how much time I spent mending and preparing clothes. In the summer of 1995 at the National Women's Conference in Columbus, Texas my friends from church selected me as their choice to win the Virtuous Woman Award. Each church group selected one person. I was surprised to receive the nice plaque which contains this as part of the inscription:

"Recognized for your Christ-like attributes, standard of integrity and an unselfish life devoted to prayer and good works."

Proverbs 31: 30-31

I was speechless. Their nomination was mainly because of the work I was doing with the Somerville Community Action Team.

To help promote community awareness we decided to enter a truck in the homecoming parade in October of 1995. We had a sign made with the full name and SCAT acronym; we taped it to the side of the truck, but who would ride in the truck?

"Okay, I will do it," I heard myself saying. I rode inside the truck with the driver and waved to everyone along the parade route. At age 79 it was my first time to be in a parade. It worked! The community did become more aware of what we were doing.

On September 10, 1996 the Somerville mayor, most local pastors, and many lay people held a meeting to organize a more sustainable assistance ministry. With the city and the different church volunteers working together it resulted in a permanent location being made available. The new ministry is called Somerville Area Assistance Ministry, therefore, SAAM. I kept the checkbook for the new group as well. Better and more detailed records allowed SAAM to avoid having people abuse the services.

This was like a dream come true. There were so many volunteers with so much "know-how." I worked with them to sort the clothes, stock shelves, and pay the bills. I was volunteering three days a week from 9:00 AM to 1:00 PM.

One day I went to get my sweater when it was time to leave. It wasn't on the back of the chair where I felt sure I had left it. I started looking around.

"What on earth are you looking for?"

"I thought I left my nice sweater right here on the back of my chair."

"What color is it?"

"Blue – sort of a light blue."

"Blue? With the pockets? Oh, no! I priced it and sold it earlier this morning! I am so sorry."

One of the new volunteers had actually sold my sweater. I finally laughed, "Do we have any more in stock? I need to buy a sweater!" We had a lot of fun working together to help the community.

It seemed that I was busier than ever or maybe it just took me longer to do things now that I was older. Whatever, I also attended weekly ladies meeting at church and participated in the prayer chain, committing time to pray for anyone who contacted the church requesting prayer. Reverend Phyllis Riney, pastor of the First Methodist Church, started a community prayer breakfast which met once a week at 7:30 AM at the Windmill Restaurant (Neinast's) in town. I participated in that every week also.

The school district was having trouble getting enough substitute teachers to cover classes when teachers were absent or out for training. I had always felt that I could have been a school teacher. I was sure that I could do it so I talked myself into applying for the job, never mind that I was now in my 80's. Substitute teaching is more about how you relate to people and manage a classroom than about teaching. I did it and I survived!

When the ministerial alliance planned an annual cross-walk to start on Good Friday of 1999, I volunteered to join the crusade. We began our march near the Lutheran Church and proceeded across town to the bank. Teenagers carrying a huge cross were at the front of our procession.

Also in April of 1999 my neighbor Marian Feick was killed in an automobile accident. LaVerne and I were returning home from College Station and hadn't gone far when we passed the awful wreck at Highway 60 and FM 2818. We later found out that it was Marian. The girls, Donna, Cathy, and Karin were now all grown up with families of their own. They came to visit and LaVerne and I attended their mom's funeral. LaVerne was now doing most of my driving away from Somerville. I still drove to town, to church, to the SAAM house, and to Caldwell to the nursing home each week. My volunteering there was now catalogued under the "Senior

Corps" which is a federal program hailed by President George W. Bush as seniors serving America on the home front.

The SAAM house Volunteers took on a project to help an Indian Reservation which is located near Rapid City, South Dakota. Needed items were collected for a year and then in August of 1999 fifteen volunteers and SAAM director Mickey Morris accompanied the eighteen-wheeler which carried clothing, school supplies, and quilts on this 1,200 mile trip. At age 83 I was the oldest volunteer to make the trip and was excited to be included. We stayed for two days to help unload the stuff and before we left all the items had been claimed.

One week-end several of my kids were at my house sitting in the living room talking and eating, probably eating some cookies and pie.

Sarah spoke, "Y'all know that Alice has that autograph of President Johnson..."

Someone interrupted, "I didn't know she had President Johnson's autograph. I thought Daddy had it."

"Daddy may have had one, I don't know about that, but Alice has the piece of her poster that he signed when he came to Somerville. I was thinking that it would be neat if she had the newspaper clipping that shows him as Vice-President turning the first shovel of dirt for Lake Somerville; she could display the autograph and the clipping in a frame together."

"Girl, I don't know where that would be," I responded.

"Daddy always saved newspaper clippings, remember? I think Daddy might be in that picture. He probably put it in that box of papers that he had."

"I know he liked to save newspaper clippings."

Sarah continued, "Do you know where that box is that he always put everything in?"

"I guess it's in the attic."

"Do you mind if I look for it?"

"No, but I'm sure it's hot up there."

Sarah accessed the attic and found the box which was still tied up with a string. Keep in mind that Hugo had died in 1972 and I don't remember if he had put the box up there or if I did it later, but it had been there a while, at least 25 years, maybe 30 years. All eyes were on Sarah as she dusted off the treasure.

"I hope it's in here!"

She untied the string and opened the "box of a thing." It really looked like an undersized briefcase that had been tied with a string because it was coming apart.

Sarah lifted out some old pamphlets. Inside were written dates and amounts of cotton picked: payday records from our cotton-pickin' days. Everyone wanted to see those. Under the pamphlets was a small notebook that looked like a snuff can.

There were several newspaper clippings, one of which was a picture of an old man that Hugo had ridden the train with. The caption said that it was Frank James, but many people thought that it was Jesse James. Sarah looked through the other newspaper clippings, but she did not find the one she wanted. The kids divided up the treasures.

"What's that other stuff?"

"Some envelopes, I guess it's some letters," Sarah opened a few of them and quickly glanced over the pages. She opened another.

"This one looks like a land deed."

Joyce said, "Let me see that." Joyce began reading and then, "My word! It's dated 1938."

Now I wanted to see it, "1938? I bet that's the land deed I was searching for; the one that never got filed with the county."

Joyce handed me the papers. Some of the words were worn, but all the important parts were clear as could be. My name was on it in four places, Nora Mae Hein, and there was my signature … and … there it was, on the last page … we had kept our mineral rights.

I knew it! It didn't change one thing about the oil money I had missed in the 1980's, but I had remembered correctly.

"We gotta' get this thing filed."

The deed had been notarized on January 26th, 1938. This was the summer of the year 2000.

Chapter 21

Shifting Down

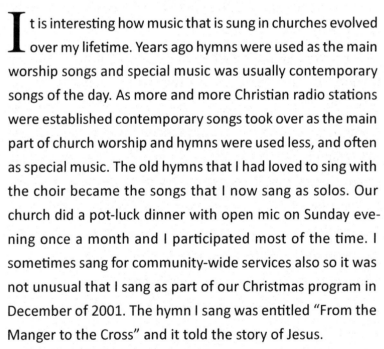

It is interesting how music that is sung in churches evolved over my lifetime. Years ago hymns were used as the main worship songs and special music was usually contemporary songs of the day. As more and more Christian radio stations were established contemporary songs took over as the main part of church worship and hymns were used less, and often as special music. The old hymns that I had loved to sing with the choir became the songs that I now sang as solos. Our church did a pot-luck dinner with open mic on Sunday evening once a month and I participated most of the time. I sometimes sang for community-wide services also so it was not unusual that I sang as part of our Christmas program in December of 2001. The hymn I sang was entitled "From the Manger to the Cross" and it told the story of Jesus.

After singing I didn't feel quite right and I went to sit on the back row in the sanctuary. Thankfully, one of the church ladies who is a nurse noticed me and came over right away.

She asked me a few simple questions and immediately suspected that I was having a heart attack. She dialed 911 and I was taken by ambulance to St. Joseph's Hospital in Bryan, a thirty mile drive. The emergency room doctors confirmed her fear.

I had experienced a major heart attack and was going to face open heart surgery if I lived. "We don't know if she'll make it," they told my family. My age was not in my favor. Hugo Jr. and LaVerne notified the rest of the family and many of my kids and grandkids headed to Bryan to join the waiting room vigil.

I will try to describe what happened. I felt myself trying to float up. In intensive care two family members were allowed to visit me for 10 minutes every two hours (I think it was every two hours). Because there were so many people in my family they would rotate in and out. Two would stay for about three minutes and then let two others come in. Every time my loved ones entered the room I could feel their love pulling on me. Almost everyone said a prayer when they came in and I was beginning to feel more and more alert. Some of the kids later told me that at first my eyes were very pale and lacked their normal sparkle. They were talking to me, but I could not respond.

With every visit I grew a bit stronger and finally managed to sit up just as one of my grandson preachers and his wife came in. He was shocked to see me sitting.

"Grandma Hein, How are you? They said you're doing bad, but you look good. I came to pray for you."

I took his hand, "I'm ready to go home. Please pray. I want you to rebuke the spirit of death that's in this room."

As I am writing this I have to laugh because it sounds as if I know all about the spirit of death and how it operates. Nothing could be farther from the truth. I am only relating my experience as an INSIGNIFICANT person who received God's grace and favor. I was not afraid to die; I just didn't want to die. There was still much work left to do and I knew that a young preacher, a man of God, had just entered my room. I also knew that I felt the spirit of death.

My grandson laughed with his little cackle that usually makes me smile, "They told me you had one foot in the grave — I don't believe that. You look so alert. I will rebuke the spirit of death."

"Spirit of Death, in Jesus' name, I rebuke you. I command you to restore Grandma Hein and leave this room."

I felt it immediately. I leaned back against the pillow and my blood seemed to replenish my entire body. I squeezed my grandson's hand. He and his wife left the room and two more visitors came in.

The next morning before surgery they checked everything again. A dramatic change had taken place! I did not need open heart surgery. They said that my heart looked like the heart of a sixty-something year old. They would only need to stent my blood vessel. I had been to the brink of death and was walking away again.

I definitely knew that I was living on borrowed time now and wanted to make the most of every day, but I sensed a bit of a slowing down within me. I could see it around me too. Sister Williams moved away to a nursing home nearer her children. (They said that she was preaching every day there to her most captive audiences ever!) In 2001 Brother Robert's wife Shirley died; my neighbor Ken Feick remarried, sold his house, and moved away. That house was torn down. In 2002 Tillie Schoppe that I always picked up for church, died and my half-brother Hubert died. My surroundings were changing.

It seemed that I was putting in more hours than ever at the nursing home, but that could have been, partly, because I was moving more slowly. I felt a bubbling joy in my spirit, but my body was wanting a decrease in activity.

I had always had a vegetable garden and flowers which I had tended in the evenings after work, and now when I got home from volunteering I usually took a brief nap before heading outside. I began to spend more time inside, painting flowers with tube paints. The patterns were the iron-on type. The church ladies group put my flower squares together and made a beautiful banner for our new church building. We moved in in 2004.

I continued to volunteer at the SAAM house. My friend Tinka Murray volunteered there as often as I did. (She would become the SAAM director when Mickey Morris died in 2006.) I was feeling that my reflexes were slowing down and that I shouldn't drive anymore so one day I said to Tinka,

"I'm going to sell my car."

"What?" she laughed and continued, "Nora Mae, how will you get to church?"

Tinka knew that I never missed any church service or function and the new church building was several miles away from my house, not two blocks away like the first building.

"The Lord will provide," was my answer.

I sold my car to one of Nell Davis' granddaughters. Even though I knew that it was the right thing to do, I had to do it quickly before I changed my mind. This would slow me down considerably. I could no longer visit the nursing home whenever I liked. Tinka lived two blocks over from me and volunteered to pick me up for church. The Lord did provide!

2004 brought another change for me because the deer tore my fence down and ruined everything in my garden. They could easily have jumped that fence. Tinka's husband Skip Murray who was the Somerville mayor came over and helped me with the mess. I decided that I would quit gardening altogether so he took the fence down to make mowing easier.

My son Tillman had battled cancer for two years. He was declared cancer free, but was hospitalized with an infected boil on his leg. He had contracted a bacteria which killed him. He was 56 years old. When Tillman died in September of

2004, for the first time I saw myself as old. I was 88 years of age, but I had always seen myself as helping the old people, now all of a sudden, maybe I was one of them. I considered that possibility and encouraged myself,

"Nora Mae, that can't be true. Remember, you are only as old as you feel."

"And how do you feel? You have aches and pains."

"Those aches and pains are not serious though. Just joint stuff. I don't really feel old."

My Senior Corps work at the nursing home ended. In 2005 I received my last volunteer pin at the Senior Corps Volunteer Appreciation Luncheon at the Hilton Hotel in Bryan. I had logged 889 volunteer hours.

I continued volunteering at SAAM. My friends gave me rides and they were so patient. I wasn't totally grounded yet.

LaVerne and I started going to the Senior Citizens' Center. I particularly liked the singings on Friday so LaVerne would drive in and accompany me. I did qualify – I turned 90 on my birthday in 2006! Actually I had qualified for a long time, I just didn't feel old enough to go.

On August the first, 2007, I was diagnosed with a tumor on my right kidney. When the doctor told me that it was cancer, I was skeptical. He said that it was a large tumor and based on his years of experience he felt sure that it was cancerous. He also told me that because of my age (91) it would not be reasonable to treat it if it was cancer so he opted to not test any of the tissue. He felt that the cure would be worse than the malady. All I know is that I never had any pain from it before or after the doctor's discovery. My friends and I prayed and this is my journal entry:

"I don't worry about it for God is in control. I know he can heal and restore. I've been healed too many times to doubt. God's will be done. I am feeling fine. I have no pain. I am just praising God for his goodness and knowledge and grace."

I do not believe that I had cancer. I do not doubt that I had a tumor, but no test ever proved it cancerous. But maybe I did have cancer. If I did, I wasn't suffering pain from it.

Life was shifting down for me. For years some of my family members had been mowing my grass. If no one came to mow it, I did it myself; but in 2007, when no one could come to do it, I hired someone to mow it. Yes, I experienced significant changes: no car, no garden, no mowing; but my inner joy still flowed.

Chapter 22

Growing Old and then the Surprise of a Lifetime

There's "slowing down" and then there's "growing old." I couldn't do it, I wouldn't do it, but now I had no choice, I was growing old. My body was deteriorating and I couldn't stop it.

My son-in-law Billy Balke died at the beginning of January in 2008. Billy had been in the Korean War and had been a voluntary fireman. He was honored for his military service and by his fire department. One of my little girls was now a widow.

On January 23rd I got up at 6:00 AM and Doris Chandler picked me up around 7:00. We went to the Top of the Hill Restaurant for our regular group prayer breakfast. We ate and we prayed. When we finished Doris went to pay for the food and I started toward the door. I fell on the concrete floor knocking myself out and breaking my left hip and shoulder.

I was taken by ambulance to St. Joseph's Hospital in Bryan, but was confused. I wasn't sure if I was dead or not. I could pinch myself on one side so I must be alive, but where was I? Maybe they thought that I was dead too. I asked the nurse,

"Is this the funeral home?"

She laughed, "If this was the funeral home, you wouldn't be talking!"

It wasn't funny to me. The doctor said it was possible that my hip had broken causing me to fall because old bones get very brittle. I had had mine for almost 92 years at the time and had been taking calcium tablets every day for many years. The hip may have broken when I hit the floor, but more than likely it broke before I fell with the arm breaking on impact. I never expected this! Sure I was moving much slower, but I had never missed a beat! Now I couldn't even move without help; I mean that I could not even roll over. I thought I might be dying. When Alice came to the hospital, I said, "If I move on up tonight," and she thought I was talking about moving to another building because they were doing construction on the hospital and had said they were going to have to move me.

I repeated, "If I move on up tonight, everything's taken care of. LaVerne and Son know all the details. But I want you to sing, 'I'll Live On' at my funeral and I didn't write that down. I want Joel to sing too."

"I'll Live On" is an old hymn that declares "when my body's slumbering in the cold, cold clay, I'll live on! Yes, I'll live on!" It goes on to say, "when the world's on fire and darkness veils the sun, I'll live on! Yes, I'll live on!" The chorus states, "Through eternity, I'll live on!"

My body may have been trying to die, but my spirit was fighting. Alice realized that I was talking about moving on up to heaven. But I didn't die. They did surgery putting a pin in my hip and they set my shoulder. I was going to have to learn everything all over again. The doctor told LaVerne that it was up to me. If I fought I would live; if I gave up, I would die.

On January 24 Dorothy's husband Arthur McManners (Mack) died. Like Billy, he, too, was a Korean veteran and was given military honors. I could not attend any of it and grieved as I faced each day, one at a time. Two of my girls were now widows, their husbands dying in the same month.

When the time came to move me to another facility the doctor wanted to move me to a place that had no Hoyer lift, the swing chair lift which is like a crane for lifting patients who cannot move themselves and sitting them in a chair or in a wheelchair. LaVerne argued for me,

"My mother is not going there. They do not have what she needs to get better. She would be totally bed-ridden there with no chance of getting better."

The doctor argued, but LaVerne wouldn't budge. He finally agreed to move me to St. Joseph Manor, a facility which did have a Hoyer lift for moving patients from bed to chair.

The family took turns staying with me. Someone camped out in my room every night for the more than 3 months that I was in the rehabilitation center. LaVerne was my mainstay with everyone else rotating. I celebrated my 92nd birthday while there. LaVerne took responsibility to bring my <u>Bible</u> and my checkbook so I could keep all payments current. In looking over my finances she discovered that I had failed to pay one of the bills several times. It was my burial policy payment! At my age, that was probably the most important payment.

"Didn't you notice that you had money left over?"

"No. If I had any extra money I probably just put it in the offering at church."

LaVerne made sure I wrote all the checks, but she let me continue to write them myself.

My friends from church were faithful to come and visit me; I missed them so much. Mariam George came several times.

"Nora Mae, do you remember the time Tim threw a dinner roll and hit you in the back of the head?"

I did remember. We were having a pot luck dinner and someone asked for a roll so Miriam's husband Tim chunked it across the room. His aim was off a bit and the thing slammed into my head.

"I do remember."

She laughed, "You were so aggravated until you found out who had thrown it. Then you just smiled and said that it was okay. Tim had you wrapped around his finger."

We both cherished the memory. Tim had died not too long after that.

My friends at SAAM brought me a special Volunteer Recognition Plaque. I did lots of therapy with the nurses and therapists who were so patient. Gradually I got better. In May I was well and mobile enough to leave the rehab center. I had always lived alone, but was now advised that my bones could break at any time so I needed a caregiver, possibly a nursing home. Definitely no more cooking for me because getting burned on a stove was a real danger.

LaVerne did a lot of research about assisted living centers and nursing homes. She told me,

"Mama, I am going to take care of you. As long as you can dress yourself and get yourself to the bathroom, I'll stay with you. If it comes to the place where you have to be lifted, I can't do that."

It was like a gift from heaven! She never told me why she decided to stay with me and I never understood, but I was thankful. Surely I could take care of myself, I always had before. Three of my half-sisters had been in the same nursing home. I didn't want to go there and LaVerne knew it. My sister who had treated me the most spitefully had died while I was in St. Joseph's Manor recouperating.

With LaVerne's generous help, I went home on the 6th of May. My world was now totally different. Caregivers came to help with my bath and my physical therapy. I was in a wheelchair most of the time. I used a walker some, but didn't trust myself with a cane much.

Like old times, my friends came to pick me up for prayer breakfast, ladies meeting, and church. I couldn't tell them, "No."

One of the strong young men (I guess he wasn't really that young, but everyone was young compared to me) told LaVerne,

"I want to pick up Mother Hein. I can come by and get her and her walker."

I didn't have the ability to say, "No," because I wanted to go. LaVerne had to step up for me and say, "No, she can't go. She could fall again."

"I have a pick-up truck. I can help her in and out and she can take the wheelchair if that is safer."

"No."

They asked repeatedly, but LaVerne knew how fragile my bones were. The doctor had warned us both. It was as if my zeal for life was outliving my body. Drat that original sin that made us mortal!

What did I miss the most as my life slowed to a snail's pace? My answer is my church. I kept praying that I could soon be back as usual. I loved the singing and the preaching. Alice and Bill did come and take me to church a few times.

Bill is big and strong and he looked out for me. LaVerne and Joyce also took me on several occasions. I was a person who had been awarded so many perfect attendance pins that I couldn't remember how many. Once I had twenty-something years straight without a miss. To not be able to go to church was a huge adjustment mentally.

"I can do all things through Christ which strengtheneth me" from Philippians 4:13 (KJV) had always been my inspiration for meeting challenges. It now helped me adjust to a new, strangely slower world.

It's funny, but it seems that it takes a lot of mental strength to grow old. There is much pleasure derived from looking back to see one's seeds of a lifetime and how they've grown, so plant well. (If you haven't planted well, you can't undo yesterday, but don't panic. Start planting good today, however old you are. You will soon see a crop of good!)

In looking back you see what you've done, but you also see your children. The eleven arrows that Hugo and I sent into the world, of course, accomplished more than the two of us. We had managers, a telephone operator, secretaries, a biological lab technician, a plumber, a bookkeeper, a real estate agent/salesman, a nurse, a teacher, and a missionary/ preacher. We've had presidents, vice-presidents, and secretaries of many organizations. Looking back I got the feeling that I, Nora Mae, did bless the world. I never did learn to make lace like Mama did, but I had produced some pretty incredible people.

I had to find new ways to spend my time. LaVerne enjoyed doing jigsaw puzzles so we usually did those in the evening. I liked to get the border pieces put together; they were the easiest to see. Joyce came to stay with me so that LaVerne could have a break and she got me into playing dominoes. It had been a very long time since I had taken time to play dominoes. I was a decent player, still enjoying anything to do with numbers. I was reading my <u>Bible</u> and praying every day just as routinely as taking my breathing treatments. The scriptures still somehow gave me an inner boost. It was like taking a vitamin.

Someone gave me a few word search books and I did those too. I couldn't enjoy doing crossword puzzles although I did try. It seemed that my vocabulary wasn't large enough to make it pleasurable. I was left with too many blanks at the end and looking for the answers in the back was no fun!

My family came to visit often. Lourene and Bubba established a routine of coming on Wednesdays and Bubba would mow the grass and then come inside so I could beat him in a few rounds of dominoes. Actually, he won as often as I did and we always ended the game with the loser spouting off about next week's competition,

"I let you win this time, but next week I won't be so generous!"

"Yeah. Dream on."

Hugo and Dolores usually came on Thursdays and Hugo did the weed eating, trimming, and whatever else was

needing done around the house. We always played dominoes too with Dolores' chatter bringing lots of cheerfulness
to the room. Occasionally a competitive attitude surfaced,
but usually her delightful play-by-play commentary on the
game kept us all laughing, win or lose.

When Sarah called in the summer of 2008 I was taken
back. She told me that she had some news she had been
holding back since September of the previous year. She
had debated not telling me at all after I fell, but her sisters
advised her to tell me. Sarah had been close to Tillman's
ex-wife and out of the blue one day she decided to try to
locate her. All we knew was that after their divorce and then
her father's death, she had returned to live in Colorado. After
researching and then following several online trails, Sarah
finally talked to her on the phone.

"I'm doing well and Jacob is doing well too."

The conversation continued with Sarah telling about her
family and Till's ex-wife laughed and said,

"I dated several men over the years, but I never let any of
them talk me into marriage again. Jacob is 28 years old now.
I am very proud of the man he has become."

She mentioned him again so Sarah asked, "Who is Jacob?"

"Jacob is Tillman's son."

"Tillman's son? We didn't know Tillman had a son!"

"You're kidding! I found out that I was pregnant when
Tillman and I were getting our divorce. I didn't tell Tillman
until after our divorce was final. Tillman did see Jacob after

he was born. We agreed to part – I would return to Colorado with Jacob and Tillman would remain in Houston. We would each let the other begin their life anew. I wouldn't press for child support if he would let us have our own life. It has been a struggle at times, but Jacob has grown to be a wonderful young man."

Sarah was shocked. When she told me, I was shaken. Could it be true? Jacob and his wife Mindy wanted to come see me. They flew into Houston and Alice and Bill brought them to visit me.

I was anxious to see this grandson that I didn't know I had. I was almost as nervous and excited as I was in the train station seventy-eight years ago when I went to meet my daddy for the first time. It was really important to me that Jacob feel loved. He couldn't meet his deceased father, but he could meet his grandmother. I was overcome with emotion. His mother came also. Jacob met most of the family when Alice had an open house and invited everyone to come and meet them. I am so thankful that I got to meet Jacob Hein. I think about him every day. His mother has done well.

Tillman went through life changes himself. Several years after the divorce he befriended a homeless preacher and an abandoned pregnant mother of three, inviting them all to live in his home. Dee Dee always said that Tillman fell in love with her children. He helped raise all four of her children, the two youngest from infant to adulthood being their baseball park dad, their provider. They both graduated high school and Cherly got married and had a baby before Tillman died. He had been a good father and grandfather.

On Easter Sunday of 2009 Joel and Mary totally blessed me. My preacher grandson came and did a service just for me – my own private Easter service! I appreciated it so much.

When SAAM had their awards in the fall they remembered me with an "Honorary Volunteer Award" plaque. The SAAM organization was thriving; they still remembered my work even though I had not been able to help them in more than a year. I was humbled and honored.

On November 22nd LaVerne took me and my wheelchair to a community Thanksgiving party at the Baptist Church. I really enjoyed it. It was wonderful, almost overwhelming. Everyone was so kind; most of the people lined up to say hello to me. Many of them I had not seen since I had fallen in January of 2008.

On Thanksgiving Day we went to Lourene and Bubba's celebration in Bellville. By God's grace I was still able to attend the Hein family reunion in June and Lourene's Thanksgiving every year. I did my therapy for a long while and tried to walk again, but I was using the walker less and less and finally only in the bathroom. The wheelchair was becoming my norm and I was thankful for it. Nellene bought and delivered to me a motorized cart (Hooveround) with the hope that I could be more mobile, particularly outside.

Chapter 23

Checking Out

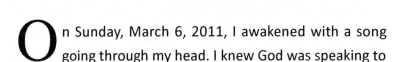

On Sunday, March 6, 2011, I awakened with a song going through my head. I knew God was speaking to me. I wrote the part I remembered in my journal.

"Death is an angel sent down from above, sent by the maker of the flowers we love.

"Gathered by angels and carried away, forever to bloom in the Master's Bouquet."

It is an old hymn entitled "Gathering Flowers for the Master's Bouquet" written by Marvin E. Baumgardner. I knew it was God's message to me that my death would not be too far away. I told Alice that now I had a different song in my heart. "I'll Live On" had been replaced.

My 95th birthday was on March 13th and the kids planned a nice party. They always had family celebrations, but some years they did large parties also including church family, neighbors, and friends. My eightieth birthday party was an especially memorable one. The family performed skits with props to demonstrate my life's events up to 1996. I wore a crown and relished every moment. This year's party was held at Mantey's Country Restaurant in Somerville with 91 family members filling up the place. Rickey's Catering did the meal for us. It was a big deal with my daughters Nell and Virginia and some of their family members coming from Arkansas and my grandchildren Byron and Shea from Florida, and Jacob and Mindy from Colorado, also making the trip to attend.

The day was complete with musical talent and a short program. We have a lot of musical talent in the family so all performances were by my kids and grandkids. When the kids each greeted me they all beamed with excitement.

"Only five years to go to 100, Mom. And then you may as well keep on going!"

Every year they encouraged me on and I always set my sights on 100, but this time I didn't feel it.

"Oh, I don't know," I responded. I was still thinking about the words to that song, "Gathered by angels and carried away..."

"Sure, Mama. You'll make it. It's only a few more years!"

How, without sounding pessimistic, do you tell someone that you know you won't live five more years? I felt that I wouldn't even have one more birthday. But I'm not God and He is the one who determines our days. Not knowing what to say without sounding pessimistic or pious, I just slowly shook my head and softly said, "I don't know."

In May I received a letter from State Senator Stephen E. Ogden. He had seen the article about my birthday celebration in *The Burleson County Tribune* and also enclosed with his letter a certificate containing the Seal of the State of Texas which had honored me before the State Senate in Austin, Texas. (Thank you, Senator Ogden.)

In June Alice came to visit and relieve LaVerne for a few days. I already knew the things I wanted her to do when she came. All of the new family pictures that I had received the past year needed to be put into my photo albums. I definitely wanted that done. I also had started a list of my furniture, listing each piece and which of my kids it would go to. Of course, if they didn't want it they could give it away or sell it, but with eleven kids it seemed to me that things would go more smoothly if I had a thorough list. And we did complete it! We went through each room in the house listing every piece of furniture and who it should go to.

Some things would obviously go to whomever had given them to me, other things took more thought. The completed list was available so everyone could go over it when they visited and express any opinion or insight. Most of my stuff wasn't worth much, but a lot of family sentiment was involved. Some furniture that the younger girls had used actually belonged to the older girls. Writing everything down was very helpful. Later, LaVerne labeled some of the antique items.

My treasures! How I had loved gathering them. Now it was almost time to disperse them. I had had such fun when Hugo and I purchased my bedroom suit, but I hadn't even used the bed in quite a while. I was now sleeping in a twin-sized hospital bed with an air mattress. It's easier on the bones when more time is spent in bed and I was getting up later now. The 5:00 AM waking time that I had kept for probably fifty years had become a thing of the past. I even stayed in bed until 9:00 AM some days and then I napped in the afternoon. It seemed unthinkable, but it was true: my body demanded more rest these days.

Coming to the end of one's journey is like ending a pregnancy. There comes a time when you can't wait to be delivered. You become very weary and look forward to what's ahead. Even if you've had a good pregnancy, your body becomes uncomfortable in the ninth month. So it is with our life on earth, it begins to take a lot of effort to maneuver through each day. Things which you have done with such ease that you never thought about them before become laborious. Things like sitting up, getting out of bed, washing your face, and even eating take a lot of effort. You are ready to pass over, but you may have to wait a bit.

I never got around to using that motorized cart, instead I found myself reminiscing often. I remembered a time when I had trouble with squirrels in my attic. Hugo Jr. had trapped some, but never got them all. We fought the squirrel battle for more than a year, and it seemed that we were losing. I finally prayed about it. One day a golden hawk nested in a large tree beside my house and before long, the squirrels disappeared. The hawk resided there for many months. Thank you, Jesus! My prayer was answered.

With delight I recalled a time when I was in my early sixties and attended a baby shower in Tomball. One of the games had been "Pin the Diaper on the Baby." Each person was timed as they folded a cloth diaper and used diaper pins to diaper a life-sized doll. I won the contest, hands down! My folding technique had given me the advantage. The young women couldn't believe how fast I was.

"I wonder how many diapers you did change!"

"Unfair! Too much experience."

They all laughed, attributing my skill to my having had so many babies of my own. And thinking of those eleven children, it is interesting to note that over a period of twenty-two years, I had given birth to eleven children. Because some of the children already had homes of their own when the others were born, all eleven were together with Hugo and I on only two occasions: in October of 1959 (I was 43 years old) and in November of 1963 (I was 47 years old). Traditionally the family got together on my birthday in March, Hein family reunion in June, Hugo's birthday in July, Somerville High School homecoming in October, at Thanksgiving, and around Christmas. Because of distance, work schedules, and their own family schedules, not everyone attended all of the functions. After Henry's death in 1966, there were no more opportunities to be altogether. All eleven of my children were together at the same time, at the same place only twice.

In July of 2011 I was dealing with a kidney infection which caused me a lot of pain and I was taking antibiotics to combat it. On Tuesday, July 19, Hugo Jr. and Dolores came over and we played dominoes. I was feeling pretty uncomfortable. When they got ready to leave, Hugo Jr. said, "We'll see you later."

There was something different about today. I gave him a serious look and responded, "Good-bye, Son."

"Oh. We'll be back again to play dominoes soon."

"I just want to tell you good-bye. Bye, Son."

Lourene and Bubba came and we played dominoes on Wednesday and I am sure I won the last game. (Well, I think I won the last game. I probably did.) I was feeling a little better.

On Thursday, Sarah arrived around 11:00 AM and LaVerne left after lunch. Dorothy was planning to come on Friday.

After supper I told Sarah that I was feeling a bit sad because it seemed that my friends had not been by in a while. I was still missing being at church every time the doors were opened. Sarah suggested that we pray together for my church friends so we prayed as we sat at the table.

"Sarah, would you like to play dominoes?"

It was the first time I had asked Sarah, as an adult, to play dominoes. During her visits we usually prayed and sang and read the <u>Bible</u> which still infused my inner being.

"Yes. We can play dominoes, but let's read the Bible first."

We read together and prayed and I was praising God for a while. Sarah put on the "Send It On Down" cd recorded by Joey and Betty Hamby. She was concerned about the volume.

"Is that too loud, Mama?"

She seemed surprised when I responded, "I can't even hear it. You need to turn it up."

She turned it up and we played dominoes as we listened to the songs: "Send It On Down," "Pulling Down The Strong Holds," "What a God You Are," "In The Presence of Jehovah," "I Worship You," "Midnight Cry," and all the rest. We had an anointed game of dominoes. It was the first time I had played dominoes with Sarah in many years. When we finished the game I felt tired,

"I am going to bed now. You need to go to bed too. You have to get up early to move your car out of the driveway in the morning, remember?"

They were working on repaving the street beside my house and a note had been left on the door that cars on our street should be moved early in the mornings or they had to remain in the driveway all day long. LaVerne had moved hers out early on Thursday.

"Yes. I do plan to do that."

On Friday Sarah woke me up around 8:00 AM so I could take my medicine. Instructions were for me to take the pill and then wait a while before eating breakfast. I got out of bed and slowly changed my clothes to get ready for the day. While I was sitting there I starting burping.

"Would you bring me a little bit of Pepsi to drink?"

"Coming."

I drank the Pepsi, but was still burping.

"I think I'll lay back down a bit." I sat on the side of the bed, "Something's not right."

"What's not right?"

"I don't know. I just don't feel right."

Sarah said, "Let's pray," and she did. "Father, we don't know what's wrong, but You do. Please give my Mama relief. Amen."

I was still sitting on the side of the bed. Sarah helped me get my feet up. They felt so heavy today. As she left the room I called after her,

"Sarah, did you remember to get your car out this morning?"

"I did."

"That's good."

Sarah went to the kitchen to answer the phone. It was 9:00 AM. LaVerne was calling to check on us, "How's it going?"

"She's burping a lot this morning."

"She does that a lot."

"She's resting now. She laid back down."

"She lays back down most mornings. Sometimes she sleeps until 10:30. I'm going outside to mow my yard. I will have my cell phone, if you need me."

"Okay. Bye."

I heard the phone ring again. It was Dorothy. She was planning on coming later.

The phone rang again. It was the doctor's office calling to see how I was doing since they had changed the antibiotic for my kidney infection.

I could hear Sarah talking on the phone, but it seemed that someone somewhere was calling my name, "Nora Mae… Nora Mae…"

"Yes?"

"Nora Mae…"

I followed the voice and walked … into eternity! "Gathered by angels and carried away" was a fitting poetic expression.

Sarah washed the sheets she had used so they would be clean for Dorothy or LaVerne, whoever would stay Friday night. She did puzzles in one of the little-used workbooks which she had recently given me. The door to my bedroom was open and from where she was sitting in the living room she could see that I was quiet and still. She put the clean sheets on the bed in the other bedroom and returned to the puzzles.

At 10:30 she came in to check on me. It looked like I was sleeping.

"Mama…Mama…"

I did not respond. She touched my arm which felt still, not yet cold. She realized that I was gone. I had routinely put on clean clothes, but this was my special day. I had left the clean clothes behind as I went to meet my maker.

Sarah sat down in the living room, thinking, "Who do I call? If she is dead, it's not really an emergency, so I won't dial 911. I will call the Sheriff's Department instead."

She called that number, but got a recording so changed her plan, "I guess I do need to call 911 after all." After that call, she called LaVerne and Hugo Jr.

An ambulance came, a policeman came, the Justice of the Peace came, Hugo Jr. came, and LaVerne came. I was dressed in my clean clothes, but the "real" me was gone. I would not greet my visitors today.

My pastor, Brother Robert, was at this time employed at Strickland's Funeral Home in Somerville. He officiated and sang at my funeral service which had several speakers and singers and then it was his job to drive the hearse to the cemetery. So after I was loaded into the vehicle, my beloved pastor took me for my last ride. INSIGNIFICANT little Nora Mae was being blessed again. God is good.

"For which cause we faint not; but though our outward man perish, yet the inward man is renewed day by day.

"For our light affliction, which is but for a moment, worketh for us a far more exceeding and eternal weight of glory;

"While we look not at the things which are seen, but at the things which are not seen: for the things which are seen are temporal, but the things which are not seen are eternal."
II Corinthians 4: 16 – 18 (KJV)

Resources

1. You Tube Video – Lesson 1
   Leavitt, Esther. "How to Tat Lesson One! By Esther."
   Online video clip. YouTube. YouTube, 1 Oct. 2012. Web.
   14 Oct. 2014.

2. You Tube Video – Lesson 2
   Leavitt, Esther. "How to Tat Lesson Two! By Esther."
   Online video clip. YouTube. YouTube, 1 Oct. 2012. Web.
   14 Oct. 2014.

3. Divine, Robert A., et al. Vol. 2 of <u>America Past and Present</u>. 2 vols.
   United States: Scott, Foresman and Company, 1984.

4. "Texas in the 1920's." www.tshaonline.org/handbook/online/articles.

5. Wikipedia contributors. "Internment of German Americans." *Wikipedia, The Free Encyclopedia*. Wikipedia, The Free Encyclopedia, 10 Nov. 2014. Web. 18 Nov. 2014.

6. Coon, Dennis. <u>Introduction to Psychology: Exploration and Application,</u>
    Fourth Edition. St. Paul, Minnesota: West Publishing Company, 1986. Pages 344-345

7. McMillen, S.I., M.D. <u>None of these Diseases</u>. New Jersey: Fleming H. Revell Company, 1971. Pages 68-74

8. Ewing, William H. <u>NIMITZ: Reflections on Pearl Harbor</u>. Texas: National
    Museum of the Pacific War, 2015. Page 12
    Scriptures labeled KJV are from the King James version of the Bible.

Descendants of Hugo and Nora Mae Corley Hein (June 28, 2015)

1. Dorothy Lee & R. Goodkouski
    Lewis R. Goodkouski
    Dorothy & Arthur E. McManners
        Arthur Nolen McManners
        Arthur E. McManners Jr. & Diane (Larson)
            Felicia & Christopher Garrett
                Briley
                Teagan
            Kyle & Brandy Larson
                Cameron Larson
            Joshua Arthur McManners

2. LaVerne Hein Chollett
    Linda Kay Chollett Leatherwood Darling
        Michael Ray Leatherwood & Chelsa Taroni
            Nickoli Stone Leatherwood

James Aaron Leatherwood & Laura Ramsahai

Andrew Lee Leatherwood

Louis Daniel Darling & Brittany Allison

Andi Annette Darling

William Hugh Darling

Alana Jayde

LH Chollett & Debra (Scott) "Debbie"

Nickolaus Allen Chollett & Amie White

Myah Suzanne Chollett

Quinn Michelle Chollett

Christopher Wayne Chollett & Erica Nicole Hemphill

Faith Nicole Chollett

Grace Marie Chollett

Mercy Kristine Chollett

Jason Davis Chollett & Olga Valerievna Gaurilova

Kathryn Suzanne Chollett

3. Nellene Marie Isom Earls

John Lawrence Zaroni "Larry" & Teresa

Derek Lawrence Perrulli

Jessica Marie Perrulli

Lloyd Frank Rabey & Sue

Brian Lloyd Rabey

Linda Darlene Isom Lynch

Timothy Lee Lynch

Charles Wayne Williamson "Sam"

David Lee Isom & Claudine

Tabiatha Necole Isom

Shelby

Patricia Ann Isom Massey

Andrew David Massey

Grace Necole Massey

Donald Mark Isom

Jash Isom

Michael Isom

Aiden Isom

Carter Isom

4. Helen Joyce m Billy Balke

Jimmie Balke m Nancy Ulstrep

Lisa Balke m Danny Thompson

Ethan Thompson

Meghan Thompson

Marleta Balke m Dwayne Payne

Amanda Payne m Nick Bofferding

Abigail Bofferding

Matthew Bofferding

Joel Bofferding

Christina Payne m Santiago Turrubiate

Noah Turrubiate

Micah Turrubiate

Naomi Turrubiate

Isaac Turrubiate

Hannah Turrubiate

Rebekah Turrubiate

Zachariah Billy Turrubiate

Robert Balke

5. Hugo Hein Jr. "Son" m Dolores Catlin

Cherie Hein m Nathan W. Sivils

Aaron Sivils

Katelyn Sivils

Joel Hein m Mary Kristof

6. Henry Roland Hein "Butch"

7. Lourene Louise m Otto Falk, Jr. "Bubba"

Cynthia Falk "Cindy"

Suzanne Falk Akram

8. Tillman Lloyd m Shirley Lechman (divorced)

Jacob Jason Hein m Miranda Genereux "Mindy"

Houston Jacob Hein

Tillman & Dolores Archer

Connie Archer m Richard Moore

Rachel Moore m Mark Figinsky

Lily Marie Figinsky

Izzy Figinski

Robert Moore

Johnny Archer

Braxton Archer

Cherly Archer m Michael Garrett

Angelina Mae Garrett

Paul Archer & fiancé Brandy Roy

Payton Archer

9. Virginia Ann m James Vaughn (Sept. 1968 to Nov. 1982)

Tracie Vaughn Perez

Shelby Perez (Leanne)

Jaden James

Kylieanna Marie

Kyson

Cassandra Cheyenne Holquin

Hope Leigh Vaughn m Russell Dallmeyer

Bailey Nicole Dallmeyer

Ty Evan Dallmeyer

Brayden James Dallmeyer

Joshua Pierson Vaughn m Katherine Seddelmeyer

Madeline Grace Vaughn

Maya Elizabeth Vaughn

Virginia Ann m Raymond Asselin (March 1983 to present)

10. Alice Faye m William Schiel "Bill"

Alyssa Schiel m Steve Hesketh

Ariah Hesketh

Sada Hesketh

William Schiel, Jr. "Billy" m Leslie Foster "JoJo"

Caulin Schiel

Jude Schiel

Grant Schiel

Ellah Schiel

Byron Schiel m Shea Cleek

Lincoln Schiel

Benjamin Schiel m Lindy Darnell

11. Sarah Jean m Neftali Muñoz

Sarah Julia Muñoz "Julie"

Nicholas Molett

Aiden Molett

Neftali Muñoz, Jr. "Lee" m Maria Isabel Quintana "Isabel"

Kendra Muñoz

CPSIA information can be obtained at www.ICGtesting.com
Printed in the USA
LVOW01s0213171015

458101LV00002B/3/P